W9-AAT-759

America's Best
QUILTING
PROJECTS

Edited by Jane Townswick

Special Feature
HOMESPUN PLAIDS

Rodale Press
Emmaus, Pennsylvania

OUR MISSION

We publish books that empower people's lives.

RODALE BOOKS

© 1996 by Rodale Press, Inc.

All rights reserved. No part of this publication may be reproduced or transmitted in any form or by any means, electronic or mechanical, including photocopy, recording, or any other information storage and retrieval system, without the written permission of the publisher.

Printed in the United States of America on acid-free ∞, recycled ♻ paper

America's Best Quilting Projects Editorial Staff
Editor: JANE TOWNSWICK
Technical Writers: GAIL GARBER, REBECCA JONMICHAELS, AND DARRA WILLIAMSON
Cover and Book Designers: LISA PALMER AND DENISE M. SHADE
Book Layout: ROBIN HEPLER
Photographer: MITCH MANDEL
Photo Stylist: MARIANNE GRAPE LAUBACH
Project Illustrator: SANDY FREEMAN
Tips and Techniques Illustrator: CHARLES METZ
Logo Designer: SANDY FREEMAN
Copy Editor: CANDACE B. LEVY
Manufacturing Coordinator: MELINDA B. RIZZO

Rodale Books
Editorial Director, Home and Garden: MARGARET LYDIC BALITAS
Managing Editor, Quilt Books: SUZANNE NELSON
Art Director, Home and Garden: MICHAEL MANDARANO
Associate Art Director, Home and Garden: MARY ELLEN FANELLI
Copy Director, Home and Garden: DOLORES PLIKAITIS
Office Manager, Home and Garden: KAREN EARL-BRAYMER
Editor-in-Chief: WILLIAM GOTTLIEB

The editors who compiled this book have tried to make all of the contents as accurate and as correct as possible. The illustrations, photographs, and text have all been carefully checked and cross-checked. However, due to the variability of materials, personal skill, and so on, Rodale Press doesn't assume any responsibility for any injuries suffered or for damages or other losses incurred that result from the material presented herein. All instructions should be carefully studied and clearly understood before beginning any project.

Photographs were taken at Harmony Barn Antiques and Country Furniture, Harmony, New Jersey, and Simon Butler Mill House, Chalfont, Pennsylvania.

On the Cover: The quilts shown are Stargazing with Roberta on page 88 and Stargazing with Roberta Miniature on page 94.

If you have any questions or comments concerning this book, please write to:
Rodale Press, Inc.
Book Readers' Service
33 East Minor Street
Emmaus, PA 18098

Library of Congress Cataloging-in-Publication Data

America's best quilting projects : special feature homespun plaids / edited by Jane Townswick.
  p. cm.
  ISBN 0–87596–707–8
  1. Quilting—Patterns. 2. Plaid. I. Townswick, Jane.
TT835.A482   1996
746.46—dc20   95–24602

Distributed in the book trade by St. Martin's Press

2 4 6 8 10 9 7 5 3 1 hardcover

Contents

Acknowledgments

August by Norma Grasse, Perkasie, Pennsylvania. Norma is a member of the Variable Star Quilters. She made August for their 1992 show, where it received first prize. She has been quilting since 1978 and particularly likes traditional quilts. Appliqué designs are especially appealing to her, because she finds them relaxing to stitch. She also likes the freedom of making a project that is not technically precise. August was shown in the 1994 American Quilter's Society show in Paducah, Kentucky, and it also appeared in the 1995 AQS Quilt Art Calendar.

Basket Pillowcases by Sandy Barford, Doylestown, Pennsylvania. Sandy designed these miniature basket pillowcases to match her bed quilt, as well as to exhibit them in the 1994 Variable Star Quilters quilt show in Harleysville, Pennsylvania. She especially enjoyed them because they gave her a chance to work in pastels, which she usually doesn't do. She has been a quilter since 1979 and loves making, collecting, and designing quilts.

Quiltote by Joanne Winn, Canton, Ohio. Joanne has been quilting since 1978. She is also a former owner of a quilt shop in Beaver Falls, Pennsylvania. Joanne has taught quiltmaking classes at quilt guilds, shops, and retreats and belongs to the T.Q.G.I.B.T. guild in Youngstown, Ohio. She creates variations on traditional patterns for her own pattern company, Canada Goose Designs. Joanne made this unique Quiltote from a pattern designed by Karen Thibert.

Pineapple Askew by Nancy Ota, San Clemente, California. Nancy made her first quilt in 1978 for her nephew's first birthday. She took a quilt class in San Juan Capistrano in 1988, after which she quickly became addicted to quilting. Nancy works as a dental assistant and is

presently active in two quilt guilds. From 1994 to 1995, she was president of the Beach Cities Quilters Guild. She loves the way that placing blocks off-center can create a wonderful feeling of movement in a quilt. Pineapple Askew was shown in the 1993 Pacific Quilt Festival, the 1994 American Quilter's Society show, and the 1994 Orange County Fair, where it won first place.

Scrapaholic's Delight by Gloria J. Evans, Naperville, Illinois. Gloria took a workshop with Wanda Hanson, whose class was inspired by reading Barbara Johannah's book *Half Square Triangles*. Gloria became fascinated with seeing how secondary patterns emerged from different placements of triangles in varied color values. She enjoys taking workshops where each student's quilt is so different from every other person's work that it's hard to believe they were made in the same class. Scrap quilts are her favorites because her three passions in quiltmaking are fabric, color, and design. She belongs to three quilt guilds, including the Prairie Star Guild in St. Charles, Illinois; Faithful Circle in Downers Grove; and Riverwalk, in Naperville. Scrapaholic's Delight appeared in the 1994 American Quilter's Society show in Paducah, Kentucky, and in the Prairie Star Show in 1994.

Twist and Shout by Sue Nickels, Ann Arbor, Michigan. Sue's inspiration for Twist and Shout came from attending a Beaver Island retreat with Gwen Marston, where she enjoyed learning freeform piecing. A quilter for more than 15 years and a member of the Greater Ann Arbor Quilt Guild, Sue focuses on machine techniques in teaching her classes and giving lectures. Twist and Shout was exhibited at the 1994 American Quilter's Society show in Paducah, Kentucky.

Grandmother's Choice by Barbara Garrett, Pottstown, Pennsylvania. Barbara had several goals in mind when she created Grandmother's Choice. She wanted to recreate the look of a 1930s quilt, include the color white plus one other color in each block, and use scrap fabrics. She has been a quilter since 1969, starting with templates and scraps from her mother's remnant basket. At that time, the hardest part of making a quilt was finding cotton fabrics for borders and backings. By the 1980s, she had developed a fascination with quilts that were popular between the 1840s and 1940s. A member of the Variable Star Quilters and Penn Oak Quilters of Doylestown, Pennsylvania, she also belongs to the Reading Berks Chapter of the Pennsylvania Guild of Craftsmen. Grandmother's Choice was exhibited in the 1994 Variable Star Quilt Show.

Yellow Monday by Elsie Moser, Dorchester, Ontario, Canada. Elsie loves designing quilts. For Yellow Monday, she made 91 blocks and, of those, selected just 64 for the final quilt. She's been a quilter for more than 12 years and is a member of the Ingersol Creative Art Centre and Oxford's Quilter's Guild. Yellow Monday was exhibited at the 1994 American Quilter's Society show, where it won best wall quilt in the Amateur Division. It also received the judges' choice award at the Canadian Quilter's Association in Halifax, Nova Scotia.

Cherry Basket by Carol B. Hood, Prescott, Arizona. A small photograph of an antique quilt in *Quilter's Newsletter Magazine* was the inspiration for Cherry Basket. Carol belongs to a quilt group that enjoys making quilts for each other. The owner of a quilt to be made by the group prepares the quilt design and buys the fabrics. Then the friends make the quilt together. Carol has been a quilter since 1979, originally quilting tops for other people in a church quilting group. She's now a member of the Mountain Top Quilters Guild in Prescott and teaches classes at a local quilt shop. Cherry Basket was exhibited at the St. Luke's Quilt Show in Prescott, the Mountain Top Quilter's Show, and the 1994 American Quilter's Society show in Paducah, Kentucky, where it placed first in the Group Division.

Tessellating Sea Horses by Donna Radner, Chevy Chase, Maryland. Donna has been a quiltmaker since 1981. Coordinated scrap quilts are her favorites because she likes to use as many fabrics as possible in her quilts. She also enjoys working out designs on a design wall, without any preplanning. She feels that working intuitively is more fun and the results are more exciting that way. Donna has done many strip-pieced, Bargello-related designs and teaches classes on both Bargello and Log Cabin quilts. Tessellating Sea Horses was shown at the 1993 Quilter's Heritage Celebration in Lancaster, Pennsylvania, and at the 1993 American Quilter's Society show in Paducah, Kentucky.

Hexagons by Betty Patty, Bradford, Ohio. Scrap quilts have appealed to Betty ever since she began to quilt in 1976, because they offer her the best way to use up excess fabric. In Hexagons, she included two of her very favorite fabrics, which she purcchased in London, England. Betty belongs to the Quilt Guild at Brukner Nature Center in a nearby area. All of the quiltmaking process appeals to her, from planning the design to taking the final stitch. Hexagons won first prize at the Heartland of America Quilt Festival in Eaton, Ohio, and it also apppeared at the 1994 Quilter's Heritage Celebration in Lancaster, Pennsylvania.

Konnichiwa by Suzanne Marshall, Clayton, Missouri. Inspired by the World's Fair block in *The Quilter's Album of Blocks and Borders* by Jinny Beyer, Suzanne added Japanese cotton *yukata* (summer kimono) fabrics, original borders, and unique quilting designs to create a scrap quilt with a geometric feel. Since starting to quilt more than 18 years ago, Suzanne has developed many of her own methods, and she likes to do all of her quilting without a frame or a hoop. Although she loves both appliqué and patchwork, appliqué has been her main focus for the past few years. Konnichiwa has appeared in many quilt shows, some of which include the 1993 Rockome Gardens Quilt Celebration in Arcola, Illinois, where it was awarded best of show. It was also shown at the 1993 AIQA Quilt Festival in Houston, Texas, where it placed third in the Traditional Pieced Division, and appeared in the 1994 Quilter's Heritage Celebration in Lancaster, Pennsylvania.

Stargazing with Roberta and **Stargazing with Roberta Miniature** by Karen Hull Sienk, Colden, New York. Karen made these quilts using many of Roberta Horton's plaid fabrics. Her employer liked the large version so much, he asked if he could purchase it from her. Not wanting to part with her quilt, Karen decided to make a smaller one in the same pattern for him. Stargazing with Roberta Miniature was the result. Karen has been a quiltmaker since 1980 and she enjoys both scrap quilts and contemporary quilts. She likes to design as she goes, without planning first. She feels that quilting is the medium through which she expresses herself artistically. She is an active member of the Southtowns Piecemakers group. Stargazing with Roberta appeared in the 1994 Quilter's Heritage Celebration in Lancaster, Pennsylvania.

Escargot in Plaid by Shelby Morris, Cartersville, Georgia. Shelby feels that she has always been a quiltmaker at heart, but she didn't actually make her first quilt until 1977. Scrap quilts are her favorites, and she loves designing machine-pieced, geometrically challenging patterns. She feels that because every quilt is a learning experience, no quilt can ever be called a failure. She belongs to the Etowah Valley Quilter's Guild in Cartersville, Georgia, which grew out of a beginner's class she taught there in 1991. Escargot in Plaid has been shown at the 1993 Georgia Celebrates Quilts show, by the East Cobb Quilter's Guild, and at the 1994 American Quilter's Society show in Paducah, Kentucky.

Homespun Baskets by Ina Sutton, Homeworth, Ohio. Ina made Homespun Baskets for a friend who is employed as a Longaberger Basket branch adviser. It was to become a sales award for one of the women in her branch. Ina likes to take traditional patterns and give them a different look. Designing and piecing are her favorite parts of quiltmaking. She thinks hand quilting is more relaxing than machine quilting because it can be difficult to wrestle with a bed-size quilt at a sewing machine. And hand quilting also gives her thinking time to plan that next project.

Ocean and Skies by Joan Dyer, Redondo Beach, California. For Ocean and Skies, Joan chose the Economy block by the Ladies Art Company 1898, as shown in *The Quilter's Album of Blocks and Borders* by Jinny Beyer. She is an active member of the South Bay Quilter's Guild in Manhattan Beach and teaches at a shop in Lorita, California. After many years as a knitter, potter, mother, and sewer, she has found her life's passion and work in quiltmaking. She feels that every aspect of her life relates to the designs in her quilts and always has at least a dozen designs in her mind at any given time. Ocean and Skies appeared in the 1993 South Bay Quilter's Guild annual show and as part of the fabric sales display of Robert Horton's fabrics at the 1994 International Spring Quilt Market in St. Louis, Missouri.

Country Wedding Ring and **Christmas Wedding Ring** by Susan Stein, St. Paul, Minnesota. The traditional Double Wedding Ring is one of Susan's favorite quilt patterns. She has made 25 of them—even one with 100 rings! She likes to combine unusual fabrics and give her quilts unique textural treatments to create special effects. Sometimes she cuts fabrics slightly off-grain for a whimsical, folk art look. She has been a quilter for 18 years and in that time has made more than 250 quilts, ranging from wallhangings to bed size. She is a member of the Minnesota Quilter's Guild and is presenty active in the Minnesota Contemporary Quilters Group. She works in a fine crafts gallery that displays quilts, weaving, and pottery and is the author of *Colorful Angles,* published by EZ International.

Plaid Folk Hearts by Roberta Horton, Berkeley, California. Roberta has been a quiltmaker for more than 25 years. During her career she has authored five quiltmaking books. She teaches and lectures internationally and, in her spare time, designs plaid and striped fabrics.

Believing that fabric is the inspiration for her quilts, she is intent on learning to listen to what it has to say, and then following those dictates.

Stars, Leaves, and Currants by Marge Karavitis, Spokane, Washington. Marge has been a quilter for more than 20 years. She likes the look of antique traditional quilts made with lots of muslin. She loves quilting so much, she makes quilt tops just to have something to quilt. For Stars, Leaves, and Currants, she combined patterns from *Treasury of American Quilts* and *Red and Green* by Jeana Kimball. Stars, Leaves, and Currants was shown in the 1991 Washington State Quilter's Show, where it won best appliqué, in the 1991 Spokane Interstate Fair, where it was awarded best of class and the Catherine Solle Memorial Award for best in arts and crafts. It also appeared in the 1991 Cheney (Washington) Show and the 1992 National Quilting Association show.

Christmas Hunter's Star by Gretchen Hudock, Singer, Wisconsin. Christmas designs are Gretchen's specialty. She also enjoys teaching beginning quilt classes because she likes to give people successful first quilt-making experiences and confidence to make more complex projects. The three-color scheme in Christmas Hunter's Star is an

especially nice one for beginners to choose, because it's easy to find a red print, a green print, and a background fabric for the Christmas holiday. Gretchen started quilting in 1984 and began publishing designs for her own pattern company, Pineberry Patch, in 1992.

Flower Basket Quilt and **Hearts and Tulips** by Cyndi Hershey, Lansdale, Pennsylvania. As owner of the Country Quilt Shop in Chalfont, Pennsylvania, Cyndi enjoys developing new projects for the classes she teaches. She often creates original designs or develops traditional patterns that have unusual or unique construction techniques. Her favorite part of quiltmaking is designing a project and choosing the colors. Cyndi has been a quilter since 1983 and is a founding member of the County Line Quilters.

Thanksgiving Wall Quilt by Kathy Berschneider, Rockford, Illinois. Kathy works as a computer aide at a local elementary school and finds sewing and quilting relaxing at the end of a workday. She has also taught classes, clerked, and made display items for a local quilt shop. She loves designing her own projects and created this original wall hanging exclusively for *America's Best Quilting Projects.* using a block called Indian Trails from *1001 Patchwork Designs* by Maggie Malone.

Introduction

One of the most enjoyable part of our jobs as quilt editors is to attend regional and national quilt shows, such as the Quilter's Heritage Celebration in Lancaster, Pennsylvania; the International Quilt Festival in Houston, Texas; and the American Quilter's Society show in Paducah, Kentucky. We look for quilts that will make your mouth water and your fingers itch to feel your rotary cutter gliding through layers of luscious prints, solids, stripes, and plaids. Trying to choose just 25 quilts to include in each new volume of *America's Best Quilting Projects* keeps getting harder and harder, because America's quilters are making more and more beautiful and sophisticated quilts than ever before.

We think you're going to adore the wide range of styles in this volume. If you're a beginner and want to start out with a quick, simple, but fabulous project, you'll love the easy shapes and surpise accent colors in Ocean and Skies (page 107). If hand appliqué is your love, you'll drool over Cherry Basket (page 57) and Stars, Leaves, and Currants (page 122); and if paper piecing is calling out to you, you're going to glory in the colorful curves and sharp points in Yellow Monday (page 46). For quilters who like traditional piecing techniques, Konnichiwa (page 80) is certain to find its way onto your "I *have* to make that one!" list. And any quilter ready for a challenge is sure to be delighted with Pineapple Askew (page 22).

Our special feature this year is homespun plaids, for which we scoured the country searching for quilts with a comfortable, country look. For example, what could be more traditional than the Double Wedding Ring pattern? You'll find a Country Wedding Ring quilt (page 112) in a stunning combination of light plaids and stripes set against a dark background. And Roberta Horton's whimsical Plaid Folk Hearts quilt (page 117) will simply beg you to cut out exuberant, free-form heart shapes from your favorite fabrics. Finally, the twirling snails in Escargot in Plaid (page 97) are bound to send you straight to your scrap bag to look for an array of shirtings, plaids, stripes—and maybe even a few snippets of colorful flannel.

To get a feel for the wide range of awards and prizes that have been given to many of these beautiful quilts, as well as a glimpse into the personal interests and backgrounds of their makers, take a few moments to read through the "Acknowledgments" section at the front of the book. This year's collection of quilts represents some of the very finest in American quiltmaking. We hope you'll find the projects of your dreams within these pages and have a great time making each and every one of them.

Jane Townswick

Jane Townswick
Editor

HEARTH
and
HOME

August

Quiltmaker: Norma Grasse

When Norma drew the month of August in her group's "Calendar Quilt Challenge," she knew exactly what she wanted to do. This original design combines two of her favorite things—sunflowers and birds—in a whimsical blend of piecework and appliqué. The result is as fresh and upbeat as a summer morning.

Skill Level: Challenging

Size: Finished quilt is 95 inches square
Finished block size is 12 inches square

Fabrics and Supplies

- ✓ 6 yards of unbleached muslin for the blocks and borders
- ✓ 3¾ yards of medium gold print fabric for the blocks, appliqués, and binding
- ✓ 2½ yards of medium green solid fabric for the bias vines and stems
- ✓ 2 yards of green small-scale floral print fabric for the sashing strips
- ✓ 2 yards of dark brown swirly print fabric for the sunflower centers
- ✓ ⅔ yard of black sprigged print fabric for the rooster appliqués
- ✓ ⅔ yard of green check print fabric for the rooster appliqués
- ✓ ⅔ yard of green and red swirly print fabric for the rooster appliqués
- ✓ ⅔ yard of brown feathery print fabric for the rooster appliqués
- ✓ ½ yard of a light gold feathery print fabric for the blocks and appliqués
- ✓ ⅓ yard of medium red dotted fabric for the rooster appliqués
- ✓ 8⅝ yards of fabric for the quilt back
- ✓ King-size batting (120 inches square)
- ✓ Rotary cutter, ruler, and mat
- ✓ 12½-inch square of tracing paper
- ✓ Black permanent marking pen
- ✓ Water-soluable marker or mechanical pencil
- ✓ Template material
- ✓ Thread to match the appliqué fabrics
- ✓ Black embroidery floss
- ✓ Embroidery needle

Cutting

Instructions are for quick cutting the background squares, bias vines and stems, sashing strips, and borders with a rotary cutter and ruler. These measurements include ¼-inch seam allowances.

Full-size patterns for all other pieces appear on pages 9–12. Transfer these patterns to template material. For instructions for making and using templates, see page 153.

Pattern pieces A, B, C, and D include ¼-inch seam allowances. If you prefer to piece the sunflower block by hand, do not include this seam allowance in the template. For hand piecing, the actual seamlines are traced onto the fabric and the seam allowances are added when cutting out each piece from the fabric.

Appliqué pieces do not include seam allowances. To cut the R-1 through R-13 pieces in reversed positions, simply flip each of these templates to the reverse side before placing it on the fabric. You may find it helpful to keep two piles of rooster fabric pieces, labeling one stack "reverse." Follow the same procedure for cutting pieces L-1 through L-3 reverse. Cut pieces in the following order:

From the unbleached muslin, cut:
- Four 13½ × 72-inch border strips
- Twelve 12½-inch square blocks
- Four 11½-inch square blocks
- 52 D pieces
- 208 C pieces

From the medium gold print, cut:
- 44 S-1 sunflower appliqués
- 208 B diamonds
- 8 R-7 and 8 R-7 reverse rooster foot appliqués
- Reserve the remaining fabric for the binding

From the medium green solid, cut:
- One 42-inch square for continuous bias vines and stems
- 8 L-1 leaf and 8 L-1 reverse leaf appliqués
- 8 L-2 leaf and 9 L-2 reverse leaf appliqués
- 19 L-3 leaf and 20 L-3 reverse leaf appliqués

From the green floral print, cut:
- Three 1½ × 72-inch strips. Cut these strips into eight 1½ × 13½-inch-long segments and eight 1½ × 11½-inch-long segments.

- Two 2 × 69½-inch sashing strips for the top and bottom sashing strips
- Six 2 × 66½-inch vertical sashing strips
- Four 2 × 63-inch strips. Cut these strips into 2 × 12½-inch sashing strips. You will need a total of 20 sashing strips.

From the dark brown swirly print, cut:
- 13 E circles for the sunflower centers in the blocks
- 44 S-2 circles for the sunflower centers in the borders

From the black sprigged print, cut:
- 8 R-2 and 8 R-2 reverse tail feather appliqués
- 8 R-4 and 8 R-4 reverse tail feather appliqués
- 8 R-6 and 8 R-6 reverse tail feather appliqués

From the green check fabric, cut:
- 8 R-1 and 8 R-1 reverse tail feather appliqués
- 8 R-3 and 8 R-3 reverse tail feather appliqués
- 8 R-5 and 8 R-5 reverse tail feather appliqués

From the red swirly print, cut:
- 8 R-8 and 8 R-8 reverse rooster chest appliqués

From the green swirly print, cut:
- 8 R-9 and 8 R-9 reverse rooster chest appliqués

From the brown feathery print, cut:
- 8 R-10 and 8 R-10 reverse rooster chest appliqués

From the light gold feathery print, cut:
- 208 A triangles
- 8 R-12 and 8 R-12 reverse rooster head appliqués

From the medium red dotted fabric, cut:
- 8 R-11 and 8 R-11 reverse rooster comb appliqués
- 8 R-13 and 8 R-13 reverse rooster comb appliqués

Piecing the Sunflower Blocks

This quilt consists of 13 pieced sunflower blocks, each with an appliquéd center circle.

1. Referring to the **Sunflower Block Diagram,** lay out 16 A triangles, 16 B diamonds, 16 C triangles, four D pieces, and one E center circle.

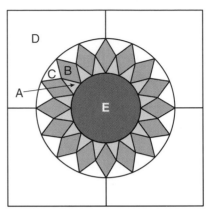

Sunflower Block Diagram

2. Sew an A triangle to a B diamond, stopping the seam ¼ inch in from the raw edge, as indicated by the dot in **Diagram 1,** to allow the subsequent C pieces to be set in easily at an angle. Make 16 of these A/B units.

Diagram 1

3. Referring to **Diagram 2,** sew these A/B units into groups of four, followed by groups of eight, and finally into the 16 units that complete the pieced portion of the sunflower. Press the seam allowances toward the A triangles.

Diagram 2

4. Insert a C piece between the points of the B diamonds, as shown in **Diagram 3.** Sew from the pivot point out to the edge of the B diamonds. Press the seam allowances toward the C pieces.

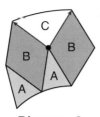

Diagram 3

5. Prepare the E center circle for hand appliqué and pin it over the center of the pieced sunflower, as shown in **Diagram 4.** Appliqué it with a blind stitch.

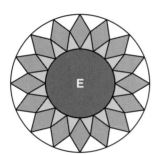

Diagram 4

6. Fold each of the D pieces in half and crease the midpoints. Match these midpoints to center B diamond in each quarter of the sunflower. Sew a D piece to each quarter, leaving a ¼ inch free at each end, as shown in **Diagram 5,** in order to complete the remaining short side seams easily. Press these seam allowances toward the D pieces.

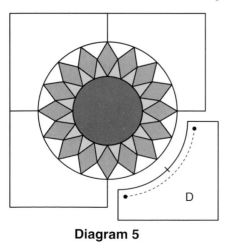

Diagram 5

7. Referring to **Diagram 5,** complete the sunflower block by sewing the remaining short side seams of the D pieces. Press these seam allowances to one side.

8. Make a total of 13 sunflower blocks.

Appliquéing the Rooster Blocks

There are twelve 12-inch appliquéd rooster blocks in the center of this quilt top. There are also four 11-inch rooster blocks at the corners of the quilt borders. Prepare and appliqué the blocks in the same manner; only the size of the muslin background square differs.

Study the quilt photograph on page 2. You will notice that in half of the blocks, the roosters face toward the right and in the other half the roosters face toward the left. In eight of the blocks, you will use pattern pieces R-1 through R-13. For the other eight blocks, use pieces R-1 reverse through R-13 reverse.

1. To make a master pattern for marking the appliqué design on the background squares, fold a 12½-inch square of tracing paper in half vertically, horizontally, and diagonally in both directions. Referring to the **Rooster Block Diagram** for the correct placement of each appliqué shape, use the appliqué templates and a mechanical pencil to draw the outlines of the rooster on the tracing paper, remembering that some of the

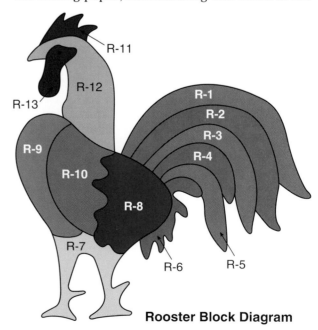

Rooster Block Diagram

pieces will overlap each other when they are stitched. When you are satisfied with the master pattern, darken the drawn lines with a black permanent marking pen and allow the ink to dry.

2. Referring to the **Rooster Block Diagram** on page 5, prepare pieces R-1 through R-13 according to your preferred method for hand appliqué.

3. Fold and lightly crease a 12½-inch background square in half vertically, horizontally, and diagonally in both directions.

4. Center the background square over the master pattern. Using a water-soluable fabric pen or a mechanical pencil, lightly transfer the pattern guidelines to the background square.

5. Referring to the **Rooster Block Diagram,** position, baste and appliqué the rooster in numerical order, beginning with R-1 and working through R-13. Note that there is no need to appliqué a seam allowance where another piece will overlap it. For more information on hand appliqué, see page 157.

6. Using three or four strands of black embriodery floss, embroider an eye on each rooster, using either a French knot or a satin stitched circle.

7. Mark and appliqué eight 12½-inch and two 11½-inch squares facing this direction.

8. For the remaining eight blocks, refer to the **Reverse Rooster Block Diagram** and flip the master pattern over before transferring the appliqué design to the background squares. This will give you a mirror image to trace onto the background squares, so that these roosters will face in the opposite direction. Remember to use appliqué pieces R-1 reverse through R-13 reverse when completing these blocks.

9. Mark and appliqué eight 12½-inch and two 11½-inch reverse squares.

Assembling the Quilt Top

1. Referring to the **Quilt Diagram,** place the twenty-five 12½-inch blocks in five vertical rows of five blocks each. Insert a 2 × 12½-inch sashing strip between each block in each row. Sew the blocks and sashing strips together to complete the rows, pressing the seam allowances away from the blocks.

2. Referring to the **Quilt Diagram,** insert a 2 × 66½-inch sashing strip between each of the vertical rows. Sew the rows and sashing strips together, aligning the blocks horizontally before pinning and stitching. Press the seam allowances toward the sashing strips.

3. Referring to the **Quilt Diagram,** sew a 2 × 66½-inch sashing strip to the left and the right edges of the quilt top. Press the seam allowances toward the sashing strips.

4. Referring to the **Quilt Diagram,** sew a 2 × 69½-inch sashing strip to both the top and bottom edges of the quilt top. Press the seam allowances toward the sashing strips.

Appliquéing the Borders

The borders in this quilt have a free-flowing, folk-art quality. At first glance, they seem to be identical, but on closer inspection, you will discover that they are not even symmetrical. So have fun creating borders similar to these, or relax and create some interestingly unique borders of your own design. A few general tips will help you get started:

Each border has a straight stem that springs up from the midpoint and it is crowned with a single appliquéd sunflower. The border vines flow somewhat symmetrically, forming a "mirror image" on either side of this central axis.

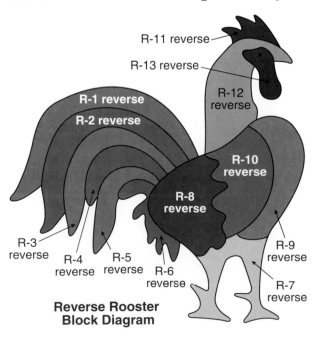

R-11 reverse
R-13 reverse
R-1 reverse
R-2 reverse
R-12 reverse
R-10 reverse
R-8 reverse
R-3 reverse
R-4 reverse
R-5 reverse
R-6 reverse
R-9 reverse
R-7 reverse

Reverse Rooster Block Diagram

Quilt Diagram

Besides this central sunflower, each border contains ten additional sunflowers placed somewhat symmetrically in groups of five on both sides.

The placement of the leaves is much more casual. The top border has 4 large L-1 leaves, 7 medium L-2 leaves, and 8 small L-3 leaves. The right border has 4 large, 1 medium, and 12 small leaves. The bottom border has 4 large, 6 medium, and 9 small leaves. The left border has 4 large, 3 medium, and 10 small leaves. Keeping in mind that these leaves are a mix of both "regular" and "reverse" leaves, you'll find there is lots of freedom for self-expression in these borders.

1. From the 42-inch square of green fabric, cut a continuous bias strip approximately 2¾ inches wide for the vines. Cut this strip into eight segments, each approximately 48 inches long. Refer to page 158 for more information on making bias strips for stems and vines. Each of these 48-inch-long vines should finish approximately 1 inch wide.

2. Cut and make 12 more bias segments that finish approximately 1 × 12 inches for the branches.

3. Cut and make 12 more bias segments that finish approximately 1 × 4 inches for the stems.

4. Cut the balance of the square into a bias strip approximately ⅞ inch wide. Divide this long strip into a total of 72 "leaf stem" segments that finish approximately ¼ × 3 inches each. Refer to page 158 for tips on using bias presser bars to make perfect narrow stems.

5. Prepare the S-1 and S-2 sunflower appliqués and all leaf appliqués, according to your preferred method of hand appliqué.

6. Measure the quilt both vertically and horizontally through the center of the quilt top. Trim the 13½ × 72-inch border strips to this measurement.

7. Fold each of the border strips in half lengthwise and crease the midpoints. Referring to the quilt photograph on page 2 and the **Quilt Diagram** on page 7, pin and baste a curving vine in either direction out from this midpoint.

8. Place a branch segment at the midpoint crease and top it with S-1 and S-2 sunflower appliqués. Place annother branch diagonally on both sides of the center branch, topping each of these branches with S-1 and S-2 sunflower appliqués. Pin or baste in place.

9. Place four sunflowers along the vine on either side of the central branch. Anchor these sunflowers to the vine with branches as desired. Note that some of the sunflowers are placed right on the vine, without branches. Pin or baste these flowers in place.

10. Scatter the leaves and leaf stems over the balance of the border vine, referring to the quilt photograph and guidelines listed earlier. Pin or baste them in place.

11. Appliqué all border leaves, sunflowers, and vines in place, tucking raw edges of all branches and stems under the appropriate sunflowers and leaves.

12. Appliqué four border panels, labeling them "top," "bottom," "left," and "right," referring to the photograph on page 2, or as desired.

Completing the Rooster Corner Squares

1. Join a 1½ × 11½-inch green sashing strip to the left and the right sides of an 11½-inch Rooster block. Press the seam allowances toward the sashing strips.

2. Sew a 1½ × 13½-inch sashing strip to the top and bottom of the block. Press the seam allowances toward the sashing strips.

3. Make four of these rooster squares for the border corners.

Attaching the Borders to the Quilt Top

1. Mark the midpoints of the "top" and "bottom" appliquéd borders and the top and bottom edges of the quilt top. Matching these midpoints, sew the appliquéd borders to the top and bottom edges of the quilt top. The central branch and sunflower in each border should point toward the outer edge of the quilt. Press the seam allowances toward the outer edges of the quilt.

2. Sew a rooster corner square to each end of the remaining two appliquéd borders, referring to the **Quilt Diagram** on page 7 for placement.

3. Sew a border strip/corner square unit to each side of the quilt, matching midpoints. Press the seams toward the outer edges of the quilt.

Quilting and Finishing

1. Mark quilting designs on the completed quilt top. The quilt shown is quilted in the ditch around each shape in the pieced sunflower, around each sashing strip, and around each appliquéd piece in both blocks and borders. There are veins quilted in each leaf and swirled lines that follow the pattern of the fabric in the center of each sunflower. Additional quilting lines are indicated on pattern D on page 12. The remaining background areas of both blocks and borders are quilted in an overall 1-inch diagonal grid.

2. Divide the backing fabric into three lengths, each measuring 44 × 103½ inches. Remove the selvages and sew the panels together along the long edges. Press the seams open.

3. Layer the quilt back, batting, and quilt top, centering the quilt top so that the seams of the quilt back will be equidistant from both the right and left sides of the quilt top. Baste; then trim the quilt back to approximately 3 inches larger than the quilt top on all sides.

4. Quilt all marked lines, adding additional quilting as desired.

5. From the medium gold binding fabric, make approximately 390 inches of double-fold, straight-grain binding. For instructions on making and attaching binding, see page 164.

6. Sew the binding to the quilt top. Trim excess batting and backing. Using thread to match the binding and an invisible appliqué stitch, hand finish the binding on the back of the quilt.

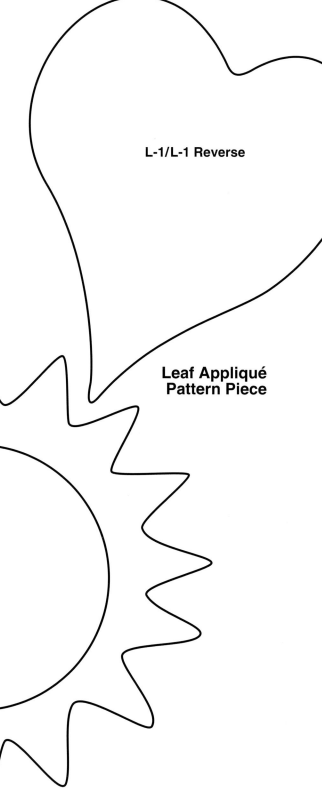

L-1/L-1 Reverse

**Leaf Appliqué
Pattern Piece**

S-2

S-1

Sunflower Appliqué Pattern Pieces

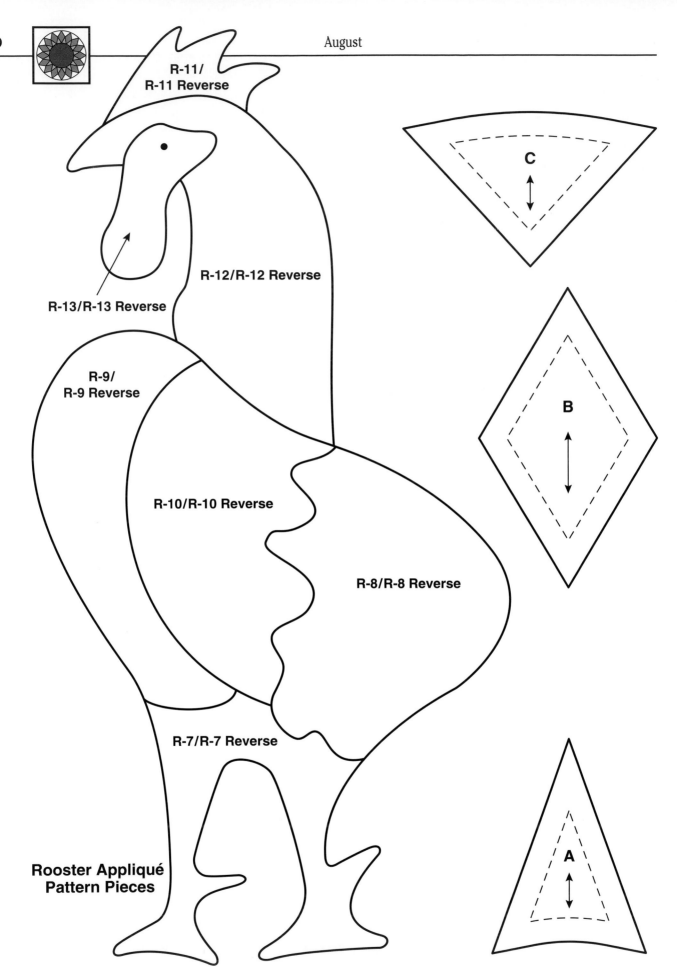

R-11/
R-11 Reverse

R-12/R-12 Reverse

R-13/R-13 Reverse

R-9/
R-9 Reverse

R-10/R-10 Reverse

R-8/R-8 Reverse

R-7/R-7 Reverse

C

B

A

Rooster Appliqué
Pattern Pieces

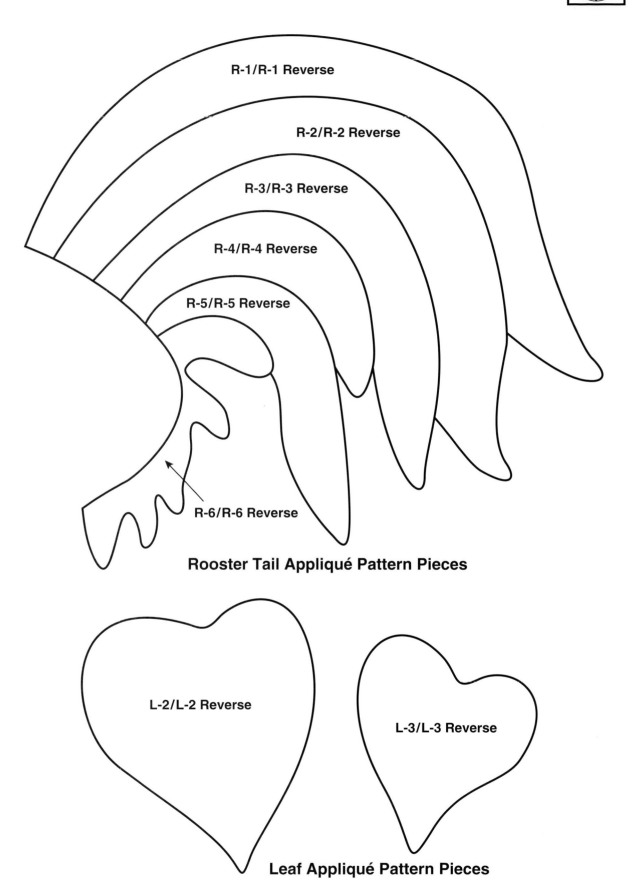

R-1/R-1 Reverse

R-2/R-2 Reverse

R-3/R-3 Reverse

R-4/R-4 Reverse

R-5/R-5 Reverse

R-6/R-6 Reverse

Rooster Tail Appliqué Pattern Pieces

L-2/L-2 Reverse

L-3/L-3 Reverse

Leaf Appliqué Pattern Pieces

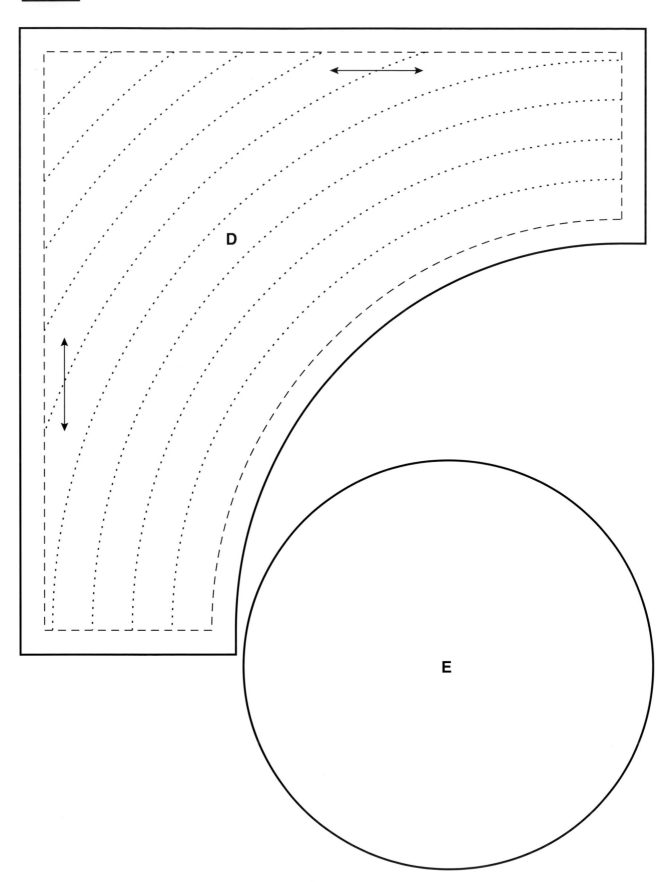

Basket Pillowcases

Quiltmaker: Sandy Barford

With pastel subtlety, Sandy created pillowcases that are as fresh as a spring breeze. The charming appliqué borders hint at flower beds and fresh buds, and the miniature basket blocks underline her garden theme. This pattern could easily be made into a wall quilt by continuing the appliqué border around all four edges.

Skill Level: Intermediate

Size: Finished pillowcase is approximately 20 × 30½ inches
Finished block is 6 inches square

Fabrics and Supplies for Two Pillowcases

✓ 1 yard of light print fabric for background, blocks, and borders

✓ ½ yard of pink print fabric for inner borders and binding

✓ ½ yard of green print fabric for the pieced sashing strips, appliquéd stems, and leaves

✓ Scraps (*each* approximately 8-inches square) of 24 different pastel print fabrics for the baskets and border appliqués

✓ 2 yards of white fabric for the pillowcase backings

✓ Template plastic

Cutting

All measurements include ¼-inch seam allowances. Measurements for the borders are longer than needed; trim them to the exact length when they are added to the pillowcase. Instructions are for quick-cutting the pieces with a rotary cutter and ruler. Note that for some of the pieces, quick-cutting and -piecing methods may result in leftovers or pieces that need to be trimmed.

From the light print fabric, cut:
- Two 5 × 22-inch strips for the appliqué borders
- Six 2 × 26-inch strips for the outer borders
- Twelve 3½-inch squares for the basket block centers
- Six 1½ × 44-inch strips for the pieced sashing strips
- Four 1⅜ × 44-inch strips. Cut these strips into 1⅜ × 3-inch D rectangles. You will need a total of 48 D rectangles.
- Two 2⅝ × 44-inch strips. Cut these strips into twenty-four 2⅝-inch squares; cut these squares in half diagonally to make 48 C triangles.

From the pink print fabric, cut:
- Eight 1½ × 25-inch strips for the inner borders
- Two 1½ × 44-inch binding strips

From the green print fabric, cut:
- Six 1½-inch × 44-inch strips for the pieced sashing strips
- 6 flower stems, using the H pattern on page 17
- 12 pieces for the leaves, using the G pattern on page 17

From each of the 24 pastel print fabric scraps, cut:
- One 3-inch square. Cut this square in half diagonally to make 2 A triangles.
- Two 1⅞-inch squares. Cut these squares in half diagonally to make 4 B triangles.
- Two 1⅛ × 3½-inch bias strips for the basket handles
- 6 different groups of 4 F pieces from 6 of the pastels for the flower petals
- 6 E pieces from yellow prints for the flower centers

From the white fabric, cut:
- Two 24 × 34-inch pieces for the pillowcase backings

Appliquéing the Handles

1. Lay a 3½-inch basket block center square over the Handle Placement Diagram on page 17. With a pencil, mark light placement lines for the basket handles. Repeat for each basket block center square.

2. Lay four pastel print A triangles around each basket block center square, using the photograph on page 13 as a guide to color placement, or experiment until you have an arrangement that pleases you.

3. Fold one 1⅛ × 3½-inch bias handle strip in half lengthwise, wrong sides together. Sew ¼ inch from the fold and trim the seam allowance to ⅛ inch. Press the strip flat, with the pressed seam allowance underneath. Shape a curve into the handle strip to prepare it for appliqué. The prepared strip will be approximately ¼ inch wide.

4. Baste the handle strip along the marked curve on a center square. Appliqué with a blind stitch, doing the inner curve first and then the outer curve, to make the handle lie flat. Remove the basting thread and repeat for the remaining handle strips on each center block. Refer to page 157 for more information on hand appliqué.

Piecing the Blocks

1. Sew A triangles to each side of a basket block center, as shown in **Diagram 1,** matching the fabric of each A triangle to the appliquéd handles. Press the seams toward the A triangles. Repeat for all basket block centers.

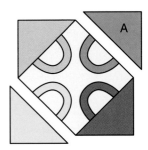

Diagram 1

2. Sew a B triangle to each end of a D rectangle, as shown in **Diagram 2.** Referring to **Diagram 1,** match the fabric of the B triangles to the appropriate basket bases in the basket block centers. Press the seams toward the B triangles. Repeat for all D rectangles.

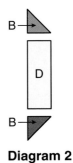

Diagram 2

3. Referring to **Diagram 3,** sew B/D strips to the appropriate sides of each basket block center. Press the seams toward the B/D strips.

4. Sew C triangles to the corners of each basket block, as shown in **Diagram 4.** Press the seams toward the C triangles. You will have a total of 12 basket blocks.

Diagram 3

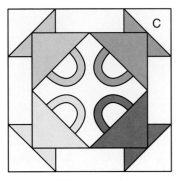

Diagram 4

Appliquéing the Border

1. Transfer the Flower Appliqué Motif on page 17 to each 5 × 22-inch appliqué border strip with a pencil. Position the pieces for each motif approximately 2 inches apart on each border and reverse the direction of the center flower, referring to the **Pillowcase Top Diagram** on page 16 as a placement guide.

2. Appliqué pieces E, F, G and H in place with a blind stitch.

Piecing the Sashing

1. Sew two 1½-inch green strips and one light print strip together into a strip set, as shown in **Diagram 5** on page 16. Press the seams toward the green fabric. Make a total of two of these strip sets. Sew two 1½-inch light print strips and one green strip together, as shown in **Diagram 5,** to make a second strip set. Press the seams toward the light print fabric. Repeat to make a total of two of these strip sets.

Pillowcase Top Diagram

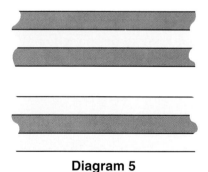

Diagram 5

2. Cut each of the strip sets into 1½-inch segments, as shown in **Diagram 6.** You will need a total of 40 segments from each color combination.

3. Alternating colors, sew two segments together end to end to make a short sashing strip, as shown in **Diagram 7.** Make a total of 16 short sashing strips.

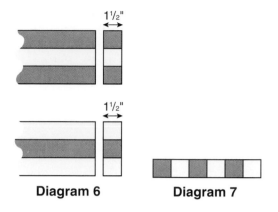

Diagram 6   **Diagram 7**

4. Alternating colors, sew eight segments together end to end to make a long sashing strip, as shown in **Diagram 8.** Make a total of six long sashing strips. Note that each will be trimmed when you add it to the pillowcase top.

Diagram 8

Assembling the Pillowcase Top

1. Referring to the **Pillowcase Top Diagram** for placement of blocks and colors in sashing strips, lay the blocks out in two vertical rows of three blocks each. Place a short sashing strip between each block as well as at the top and bottom edges of the blocks.

2. Referring to the **Pillowcase Top Diagram** for color placement, place long sashing strips between and at the sides of the rows of blocks. Remove the two unneeded squares from each long sashing strip after determining the correct color placement.

3. Sew the blocks and the short sashing strips together into vertical rows. Press the seams toward the sashing strips.

4. Sew the long sashing strips to the vertical rows of blocks. Press the seams toward the sashing strips.

5. Measure the length of the pillowcase top. Trim two 1½ × 25-inch pink print inner borders to this measurement and sew them to the side edges. Press the seams toward the border.

6. Measure the width of the pillowcase top, including the borders. Trim the remaining two pink inner border strips to this measurement and sew them to the top and bottom edges of the pillowcase top. Press the seams toward the borders.

7. In the same manner, sew the 2 × 26-inch light print outer borders to the side edges and press the seams toward the borders. Sew the remaining two outer border strip to one end and the appliqué border to the other. Press the seams toward the borders.

8. Repeat Steps 1 through 7 to assemble the second pillowcase top.

Finishing

1. Trim the pieces of white backing fabric to match the size of each completed pillowcase top.

2. Pin the pillowcase top and the backing right sides together. Sew along two sides and one end, using a ¼-inch seam allowance. Leave the appliqué border end open. Turn the pillowcase right side out and press.

3. Make 90 inches of double-fold binding from the pink print fabric. Bind the border edge of the pillowcase and sew the binding to the wrong side with a blind stitch. For more instructions on making and attaching binding, see page 164.

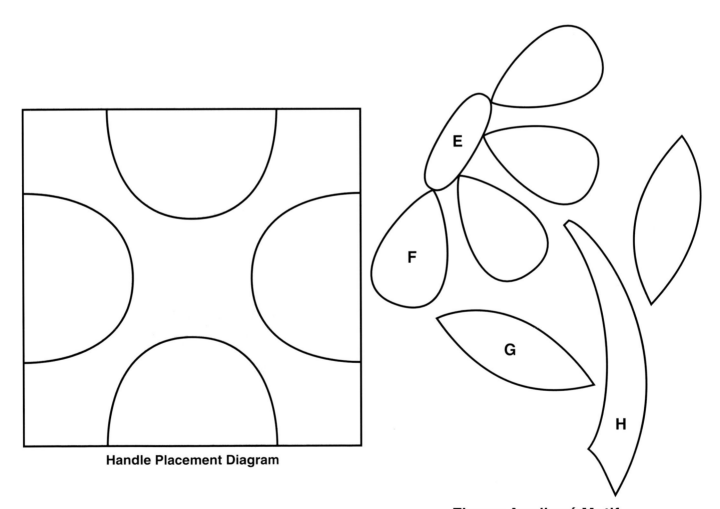

Handle Placement Diagram

Flower Appliqué Motif

Quiltote

Quiltmaker: Joanne Winn

A quilt teacher who travels widely, Joanne likes to carry her sample projects in a handy bag that will fit perfectly into the overhead compartment on an airplane. This soft tote holds a queen-size quilt and takes only a couple of hours to make. In bright, primary colors, it would also make a great bag for a child to take to a slumber party.

Skill Level: Easy

Size: Finished tote is approximately 24 inches long and 10 inches in diameter

Fabrics and Supplies

✓ 1⅜ yards of white and burgundy print fabric for the bag, pocket, and handles

✓ 1⅛ yards of burgundy print fabric for the bag lining, pocket lining, and drawstrings

✓ One 24-inch khaki separating zipper

✓ ¼ yard of 45-inch-wide Pellon fleece for the handles

✓ One 8-inch strip of hook-and-loop tape for the pocket

Cutting

All measurements include ¼-inch seam allowances, unless otherwise noted.

From the white-and-burgundy print fabric, cut:
• One 31 × 36-inch rectangle for the bag front

• Three 4 × 44-inch strips for the handles

• One 7½ × 10-inch rectangle for the pocket front

• One 10 × 10½-inch rectangle for the pocket back

From the burgundy print fabric, cut:
• One 31 × 36-inch rectangle for the bag lining

• One 7½ × 10-inch rectangle for the pocket front lining

• One 10 × 10½-inch rectangle for the pocket back lining

From the fleece, cut:
• Three 2 × 44-inch strips for the handles

Making the Handles

1. Cut one of the 4 × 44-inch white and burgundy strips in half to make a 4 × 22-inch strip. Using ½-inch seam allowances, sew the short ends of this strip and two 4 × 44-inch strips together to make one continuous handle loop. Be careful not to let the strips twist as you sew. Press the seams open.

2. From one of the three fleece handle strips, cut a 21-inch length. Discard the remainder of that strip. Abut the short ends of the three strips and baste them together with a zigzag stitch, creating one continuous loop of fleece that is the same length as the handle loop.

Tip: *Pellon fleece washes well and it provides durability in the handles of this tote. If you would like your bag to have an even thicker handle that can take many washings, try substituting a heavier piece of cotton fabric, such as denim or twill, to add more weight.* ★

3. Fold over one edge of the handle loop ½ inch, wrong sides together, and press. Fold the other edge of the handle fabric over 1 inch, wrong sides together, and press. Open up the handle loop and lay the fleece loop at the center of the handle loop, just along the line that was pressed 1 inch from the edge. Fold this 1-inch portion of the handle fabric over the fleece. Then overlap it with the other folded edge of the handle fabric. Press the entire handle and set it aside.

Making the Quiltote

1. Referring to **Diagram 1** on page 20, use chalk or pencil to mark the placement lines for the casings 1½ inch in from each edge on the right side of the 31 × 36-inch bag front. Mark two more casing lines 1¼ inches in from these lines, as shown.

2. Referring to **Diagram 1,** mark the placement lines for the handles 6 inches in from each side and 5 inches in from each long edge of the bag front. Mark the midpoint of each of these lines.

3. Referring to **Diagram 1,** mark the pocket placement lines 5 inches down from the midpoint of the top long edge, as shown.

4. Separate the zipper and baste each half face down, along the 36-inch edges of the bag front. Check to make sure that the edges of the bag front match, both above and below the zipper, and that the zipper teeth face the same direction.

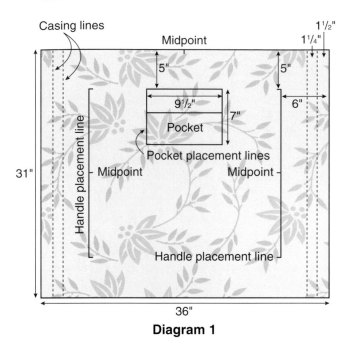

Diagram 1

5. Pin the 31 × 36-inch burgundy lining fabric to the bag front right sides together, with half of the zipper sandwiched between the two layers on each long side. Sew each long side of the bag together, as shown in **Diagram 2,** using a ¼-inch seam allowance and leaving an opening above and below the zipper. Turn the bag to the right side through one of the openings.

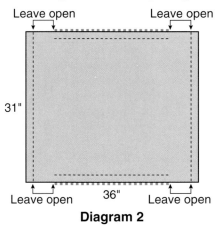

Diagram 2

6. Press, turning the seam allowance of the openings to the inside of the bag. Referring to **Diagram 1,** sew two rows of stitching to create the casings at each end. Topstitch along each zipper edge between the casing seams. Be careful not to sew across the casing openings.

7. Fold the handle loop in half and place a pin at the midpoints. Match the midpoints of the

handle loop to the midpoints on the bag front, as shown in **Diagram 3.** Pin the handle along the handle placement lines, stopping at the top placement lines. Check to make sure that the handle does not twist and that the loose portions of the handle are the same length.

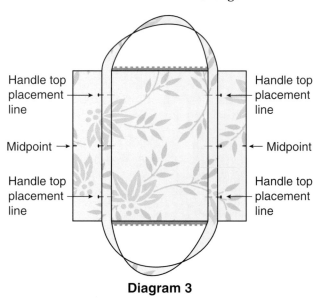

Diagram 3

8. Remove the pins at the handle top placement lines on one side of the bag. Topstitch from this point down the center of the loose handle to the top placement line below the other end of the zipper. Repeat for the loose portion of the handle on the other side of the bag.

9. In the same manner, edge stitch both sides of each loose handle. Then add two more rows of topstitching between the edge stitches and the center stitching on each handle.

10. Clip the threads and repin the loose handles to the handle top placement lines on both sides of the bag. Attach the rest of the handle to the bag by connecting the previous rows of stitching across the bag front. Reinforce each handle by sewing across it at each of the top placement lines.

Making the Pocket

1. With right sides together, sew the pocket front to the pocket front lining, as shown in **Diagram 4,** leaving a 4-inch opening for turning along one long side. Trim corners, turn to the right side, and press.

2. Referring to **Diagram 4,** sew the pocket back to the pocket back lining. Topstitch ¼ inch in from the edges on both the pocket front and the pocket back.

3. Referring to **Diagram 5,** sew the hook portion of the hook-and-loop tape to the lining side of the pocket back, placing it 1 inch from one long edge. Sew the loop portion of the tape 1 inch from the edge of the right side of the pocket front, as shown.

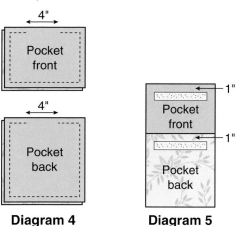

Diagram 4   **Diagram 5**

4. Referring to **Diagram 1,** lay the pocket back with the lining up at the pocket markings on the bag front. Place the pocket front over the pocket back, matching the bottom and side edges. Pin both portions in place and attach the pocket to the bag front by sewing over the topstitched lines along the sides and bottom edge.

Making the Drawstrings

1. Fold one of the 2 × 36-inch burgundy strips in half lengthwise, with wrong sides together. Using a ¼-inch seam allowance, sew the short ends and long edges together, leaving a 2-inch opening at the center of the strip for turning. Turn the strip right side out through the opening; press it and sew the opening closed by hand. Repeat to make a second drawstring.

2. Thread the drawstrings through the casings and make a knot 1 inch from the end of each drawstring.

Pineapple Askew

Quiltmaker: Nancy Ota

The twenty-first century seems just a heartbeat away when quiltmakers call on modern technology to experiment with favorite traditional nineteenth-century block designs. With the assistance of a computer, Nancy has created a dramatic, asymmetrical look in her Pineapple quilt.

Skill Level: Challenging

Size: Finished quilt is 59½ inches square
Finished block is 7 inches square

Fabrics and Supplies

This quilt takes advantage of an unusual off-the-bolt multicolored print in the blocks and narrow borders. This print contains areas of yellow, orange, blue, green, and rose that blend and flow together. The way the quiltmaker cut it gives the illusion that many fabrics are used throughout the blocks. If you are unable to locate this type of fabric, you can easily substitute hand-dyed or other commercial prints to achieve a similar appearance in your quilt.

- ✓ 4¼ yards of chocolate brown swirly print fabric for the blocks and borders
- ✓ 1¾ yards of a multicolored, blended print fabric for the blocks and narrow border
- ✓ 1½ yards of blue/violet mottled print fabric for the blocks
- ✓ ½ yard of deep brown/black print fabric for the binding
- ✓ ½ yard of dark purple solid fabric for the blocks
- ✓ 3¾ yards of fabric for the quilt back
- ✓ Twin-size quilt batting (72 × 90 inches)
- ✓ Rotary cutter, ruler, and mat
- ✓ Approximately 60 sheets of 8½ × 11-inch tracing paper

Cutting

Instructions are for quick cutting all of the block pieces and border strips with a rotary cutter and ruler. These measurements include ¼-inch seam allowances. Measurements for the border strips are longer than needed; trim them to the exact length when adding them to the quilt top. The blocks are made from strips cut in two different widths. However, to make the cutting process easier, all of the strips are cut to the same 1¾-inch width. Paper piecing allows you to trim strips to the correct length and width as you add them to the paper foundations. The number

of strips listed is only approximate because of the unusual type of multicolored print fabric used. The yardages are generous enough so that you can cut a few additional strips if you wish to include more pieces of a particular color in your own quilt.

From the chocolate brown swirly print fabric, cut:
- One 42 × 63-inch length. Cut this length into four 5½ × 63-inch strips for the outer borders and four 1½ × 63-inch strips for the inner borders.
- One 42 × 90-inch length. Cut this length into fifty-one 1¾ × 42-inch strips for the blocks.

From the multicolored print fabric, cut:
- Four ¾ × 63-inch strips for the narrow borders
- Three 2¼ × 39-inch crosswise strips for the blocks. These strips will be cut into 2¼-inch squares after the desired color placement is determined.
- Twenty-two 1¾ × 39-inch crosswise strips for the blocks

From the blue/violet mottled print fabric, cut:
- Twenty-eight 1¾ × 42-inch strips for the blocks

From the deep brown/black print fabric, cut:
- Six 2½ × 42-inch strips for the binding

From the dark purple solid fabric, cut:
- Eight 1¾ × 42-inch strips for the blocks

Color Placement in the Pineapple Blocks

There are basically just two different fabric arrangements needed for the 36 blocks in this quilt, as shown in **Block Diagram 1** and **Block Diagram 2** on page 24. The numbered piecing sequence is indicated on each block diagram, and it is the same for each block. However, each block highlights a different color from the multicolored print fabric, so for easy reference, see the "Featured Color Chart" on page 24, which lists the number of Block 1s and Block 2s to make in each of the featured colors. Refer to this chart often as you piece the 7-inch blocks. It will also be useful when piecing the border units.

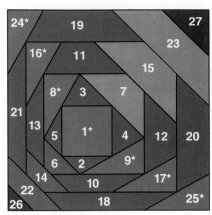

*Featured color

Block 1 Diagram

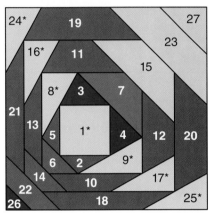

*Featured color

Block 2 Diagram

FEATURED COLOR CHART

Make the indicated number of blocks or units using the following colors in the featured color positions. The block diagrams indicate clearly where to place these featured colors.

Number of Blocks	Featured Color
Block 1	
14	Blue-green
10	Yellow-green
5	Yellow-orange
1	Red-orange
1	Red
1	Red-violet
Block 2	
3	Yellow-green
1	Blue-green
Border Unit	
7	Blue-green
3	Yellow-green
1	Yellow-orange
1	Red-orange
Border Unit Reversed	
8	Blue-green
2	Yellow-green
1	Yellow-orange
1	Red

Preparing the Paper Foundations

This quilt consists of thirty-six 7-inch blocks, 12 border units, 12 border units reversed, and four small border corner blocks, each of which is pieced on a tracing paper foundation.

1. To make the tracing paper foundations for the 7-inch blocks, start by making five photocopies of the 7-inch Pineapple Block Foundation Pattern on page 30, checking to make sure that they are 100 percent accurate in size.

2. Layer eight sheets of tracing paper underneath one of the photocopies and staple all of the edges together to hold them securely in place.

3. With a short to medium stitch length and no thread on top or in the bobbin of your sewing machine, stitch over the lines of the photocopied block foundation pattern. This will perforate all of the tracing paper at once, creating eight identical paper foundations. Repeat this process with the remaining four photocopied foundation patterns to make a total of 40 tracing paper foundations.

4. In the same manner, make tracing paper foundations for the 12 border units and for the 12 border units reversed, using the full-size Border Unit Foundation Pattern and Border Unit Reversed Foundation Pattern shown on page 29.

5. In the same manner, make tracing paper foundations for the four small border corner blocks, using the full-size Border Corner Block Foundation Pattern shown on page 28.

PHOTOCOPIES AND HOT IRONS DON'T MIX!

From using photocopied paper foundations to piece quilts, Nancy Ola discovered that the bottom of her iron sometimes became stained and that smudged areas were also beginning to appear on some of her fabrics. Her son, Chris, helped her discover the reason. Photocopies actually consist of minute particles of plastic, which are transferred to the paper during the photocopying process. If a heated iron is placed over a photocopied image, it can easily melt those tiny bits of plastic onto both itself and a piece of fabric. Nancy's solution is to place an accurately sized photocopy of a quilt block over several layers of tracing paper. She then stitches over the photocopy with an unthreaded sewing machine, perforating the sewing lines of the quilt block. Then she discards the photocopy and uses only the perforated tracing paper foundations for paper piecing her quilts. ◆

Piecing the Pineapple Blocks

The 36 asymmetrical blocks in this quilt are pieced from the center square outward, in the numerical sequence shown in the **Block 1 Diagram** and **Block 2 Diagram.**

1. For Block 1, check the "Featured Color Chart" and select the featured color for each block. Start by cutting a 2¼-inch square of the appropriate color from the 2¼-inch strip of multicolored print fabric.

2. Referring to the block diagram for the piecing sequence, place a featured print center square right side up over square 1 on the tracing paper foundation. Center the square so that its ¼-inch seam allowances extend beyond the perforated lines. Pin the featured color center square on the side of the paper foundation you will be sewing on.

3. Referring to **Block 1 Diagram,** place a 1¾-inch chocolate brown strip right sides together

along one side of the center square, aligning the edges. Insert a pin at each end to help in aligning the strip with the center square. Check to make sure that this strip is straight, that it covers all the necessary lines, and that there is ample seam allowance. Pin the strip in place. You may wish to trim it to a manageable length, remembering to allow for the ¼-inch seam allowances needed.

4. Adjust your sewing machine to 14 to 18 stitches per inch. Flip the paper foundation so the fabric side is facing down and the plain paper side is facing up. Stitch along the line between piece 1 and 2. Start sewing a bit before the fabric and sew directly on tracing paper seam line to a point beyond the edge of the fabric.

5. Make sure that the strip is sewn straight and then trim the seam allowance to ¼ inch. Open the strip and finger press it flat.

6. Trim the unsewn edge of the chocolate brown strip at the angles indicated by the lines on the tracing paper foundation, making sure to allow ¼-inch seam allowances.

7. In the same manner, referring to the piecing sequence in **Block 1 Diagram,** add a chocolate brown strip in positions 3, 4, and 5.

8. Continue to construct the block by adding appropriately colored strips, referring to the piecing sequence in **Block 1 Diagram.** Continue to finger press the seams flat and trim the strips, allowing for the ¼-inch seam allowances as needed.

FOUNDATIONS WITH EXTRA GRIP

Use the underside of the needlepunched tracing paper foundation as the side to which you pin fabrics. This is the side where the sewing machine needle comes out as it "stitches" through the tracing paper to perforate the seam lines. These tiny holes will be slightly raised or bumpy on the underside, and this texture can help hold fabrics in place as you foundation piece. ◆

9. Make a total of 32 Block 1s, referring to the "Featured Color Chart" on page 24 as needed. Do not remove the tracing paper foundations from the blocks at this time.

10. In the same manner, make four Block 2s, referring to the "Featured Color Chart" on page 24 and **Block 2 Diagram** on page 24 for correct color placements. Do not remove the tracing paper foundations at this time.

Assembling the Quilt Top

1. Referring to the **Quilt Diagram** and the quilt photograph on page 22, place the 36 blocks in six horizontal rows of six blocks each.

2. Sew the blocks together into rows, pinning generously to match seams and corners. Press the seams open to reduce the bulk, if desired. Do not remove the tracing paper foundations at this time.

3. Sew the six rows of blocks together, pressing the seam allowances in alternate directions, or open if desired, to reduce bulk.

Piecing the Border Units

There are 24 pieced border units and four corner squares that complete the quilt top. They are pieced on tracing paper foundations in the same manner as the 7-inch blocks were.

R = Border unit reversed

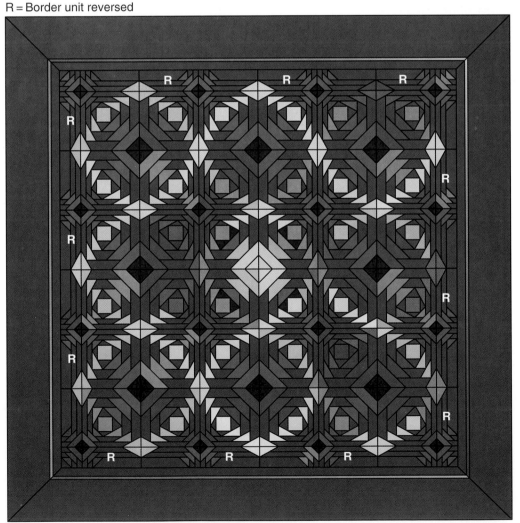

Quilt Diagram

Referring to the **Border Unit Diagram** for color placement and the numbered piecing sequence, piece the border units. The "Featured Color Chart" on page 24 indicates how many border units to make in each featured color. Finger press and trim the seam allowances as you sew. Make a total of 12 border units and 12 border units reversed. Do not remove the tracing paper foundations at this time.

*Featured color

Border Unit

Border Unit Reversed

Border Unit Diagram

Piecing Border Corner Squares

Referring to the **Border Corner Block Diagram** for color placement and the piecing sequence, make four border corner blocks. Do not remove the tracing paper foundations at this time.

Border Corner Block Diagram

Attaching the Pieced Borders to the Quilt Top

1. Referring to the **Quilt Diagram** for color placement, sew six border units together to make the pieced border for each side of the quilt top.

2. Lay out a pieced border at the top and bottom edge of each side of the quilt top.

3. Sew the top and bottom pieced borders to the quilt top, pinning carefully to match seams. Press the seam allowances toward the top edge of the quilt.

4. Sew a border corner block to each end of the remaining two border strips. Place a strip at each side edge of the quilt top.

5. Sew the side borders to the quilt top, pinning carefully to match seams. Press the seam allowances toward the border strips.

Assembling and Attaching the Outer Borders

1. To make the outer borders, refer to the **Quilt Diagram** and sew together a $1\frac{1}{2} \times 63$-inch brown border strip, a $\frac{3}{4} \times 63$-inch multicolored border strip, and a $5\frac{1}{2} \times 63$-inch chocolate brown border strip. Press all of the seam allowances away from the multicolored strip. Make four outer border units.

2. Crease the midpoint of each outer border unit and place a pin at the midpoint on each side of the quilt top. Referring to the **Quilt Diagram,** sew the borders to the quilt top, beginning and ending each seam $\frac{1}{4}$ inch from the edge of the quilt top and mitering the corner seams. Press the corner seams open and trim the excess fabric. For more information on mitering, see page 166.

Quilting and Finishing

1. Carefully remove all of the tracing paper foundations. Starting with the center square of each block, use a seam ripper to gently loosen the tracing paper. Tweezers are also helpful for removing paper foundations.

2. Mark quilting designs as desired. The quilt shown is quilted in an overall pattern that runs through the center of each block, as indicated in the **Quilting Diagram** on page 28.

3. Divide the backing fabric into two equal $1\frac{7}{8}$-yard lengths and remove the selvages. Sew the two pieces of fabric together along the long edges and press this seam open.

4. Layer the quilt back, batting, and quilt top. The seam in the quilt back should be centered under the quilt top. Baste; then trim the quilt back and batting to approximately 3 inches larger than the quilt top on all sides.

5. Quilt all marked designs, adding any additional quilting as desired.

6. From the 2½ × 42-inch dark brown strips, make approximately 250 inches of double-fold, straight-grain binding. See page 164 for information on making and attaching binding.

7. Sew the binding to the quilt top. Trim the excess backing and batting, and use matching thread and an invisible stitch to hand finish the binding on the back of the quilt.

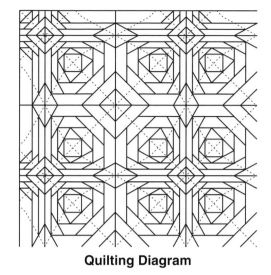

Quilting Diagram

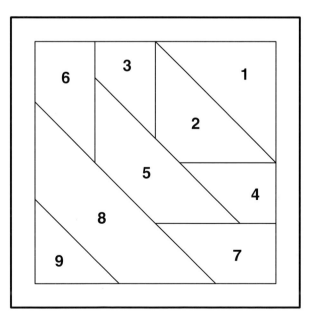

Border Corner Block Foundation Pattern

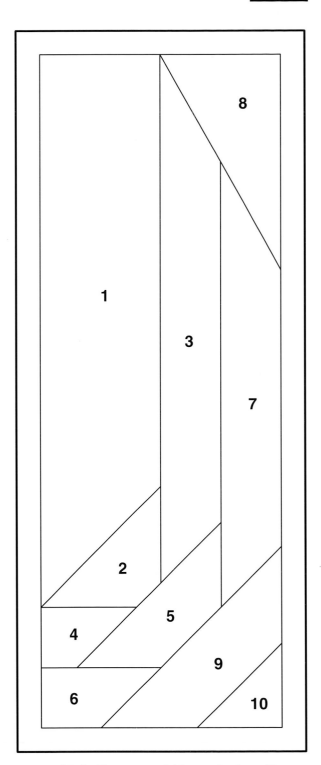

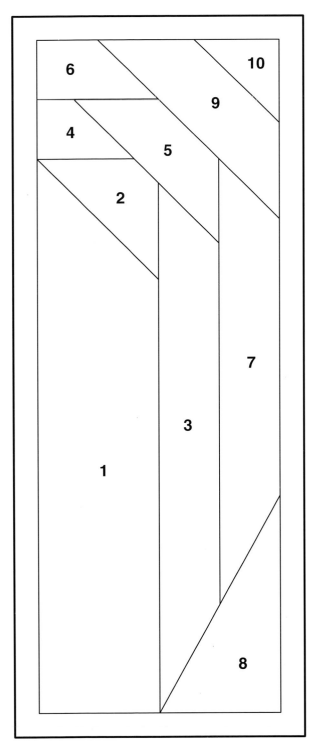

Border Unit Foundation Pattern

Border Unit Reversed Foundation Pattern

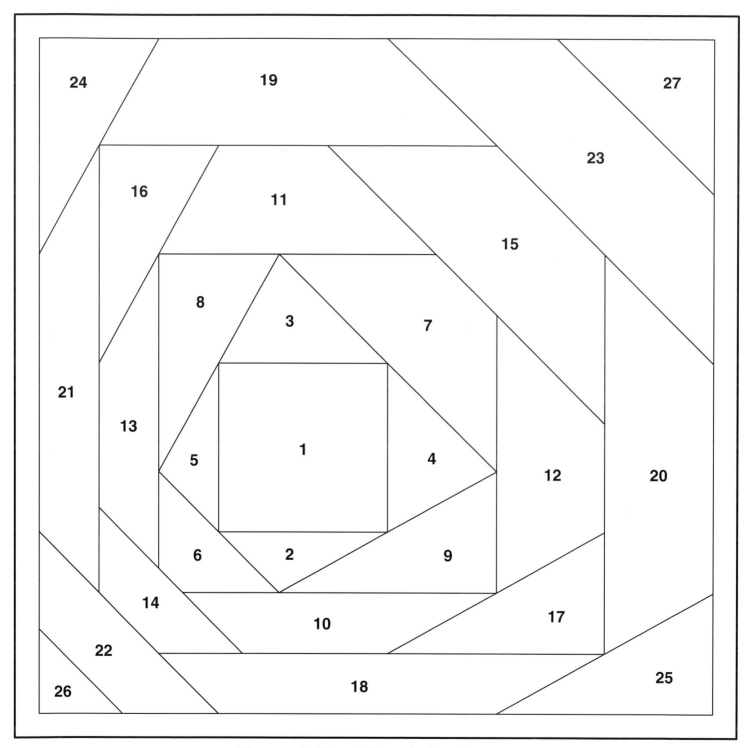

Pineapple Block Foundation Pattern

Scrapaholic's Delight

Quiltmaker: Gloria J. Evans

Does your scrap bag overflow? If so, this exuberant quilt is just what the doctor ordered! Although the entire quilt is pieced using only one triangle shape, it takes on a startling complexity through careful placement of light, medium, and dark values. Gloria's blend of sumptuous prints and solids makes this quilt a visual feast.

Skill Level: Easy

Size: Finished quilt is 65 × 85 inches
Finished block is 20 inches square

Fabrics and Supplies

The beauty of this quilt stems partially from the many visual textures in its fabrics. *Visual texture* refers to the effects created by pattern and other design elements in any fabric. For example, some prints may feature very large and splashy designs, while other fabrics contain smaller, or more delicate motifs. To consider how differences in visual texture are able to create effective contrast in a quilt, think about how a blended, overall leaf print would stand out against an evenly spaced, pencil-thin striped fabric, even if both were in the same color value. As you gather together scrap fabrics for your quilt, think of visual texture as a design tool and look for lots of interesting fabrics in varying visual textures as well as in different color values.

✓ A wide variety of light print fabrics *totaling* approximately 2 yards for the blocks

✓ A wide variety of medium print fabrics *totaling* approximately 2 yards for the blocks

✓ A wide variety of dark print fabrics *totaling* approximately 2 yards for the blocks

✓ ⅛ yard of fuchsia print fabric for the binding

✓ 5¼ yards of fabric for the quilt back

✓ Full-size quilt batting (81 × 96 inches)

✓ Rotary cutter, ruler and mat

Cutting

Instructions are for quick cutting the triangles with a rotary cutter and ruler. These measurements include ¼-inch seam allowances.

From the light, medium, and dark fabrics, cut:
• Eight hundred eighty four 3⅜-inch squares. Cut these squares in half diagonally to make 1,768 triangles.

Before You Begin Piecing

This quilt consists of 12 blocks and a pieced outer border that completes the visual pattern in each block. Each of the 12 blocks contains 64 squares, which are simply two triangles of different values sewn together. Each block contains 32 light/dark triangle-pieced squares, 8 light/medium triangle-pieced squares, and 24 medium/dark triangle-pieced squares.

Before you begin making the blocks, sort all of the cut triangles into three stacks of light, medium, and dark. Don't labor over this process; just try to get an idea of each fabric's color value. The overall pattern of the quilt will emerge through careful placement of lights, mediums, and darks. Color value is relative, because the lightness or darkness of the triangles in these blocks will ultimately depend on the values of the triangles you place around them.

Piecing the Blocks

1. As you follow the piecing instructions for the 12 blocks in this quilt, refer to the **Block Diagram** and the "Color Value Key" as a guide to the correct color placement of the 128 triangles.

Tip: *The A/A units will be more accurate if you sew the A/A triangle-pieced squares together first into groups of two, then four, and finally eight, rather than into one long, continuous chain.*★

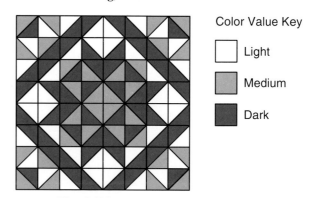

Block Diagram

Color Value Key

☐ Light

▨ Medium

■ Dark

2. Referring to **Diagram 1**, sew the first two A triangles at the top left corner of the block. Sew the bias edges together, forming an A/A triangle-pieced square, as shown. Press the seam allowance toward the darker fabric and return this triangle-pieced square to its proper position in the row. Repeat for each pair of A triangles in the top row of the block, as shown.

Diagram 1

3. Referring to **Diagram 1,** sew the eight pairs of triangle-pieced squares together, completing the top row of the block. Press the seam allowances in alternating directions between the triangle-pieced squares.

4. Referring to the **Block Diagram,** sew the remaining rows of the block together in the same manner. Press the seam allowances in alternating directions from row to row. Do not press the seam allowances in the completed block at this time.

Assembling the Quilt Top

1. Lay out the 12 blocks in four horizontal rows of 3 blocks each, referring to the **Quilt Diagram** on page 34 and the photograph on page 31 for guidance in color placement.

2. Sew the blocks together into four horizontal rows, being careful to line up the individual squares. Press the seam allowances in opposite directions between blocks.

3. Sew the four rows together, pinning carefully to match seams. Press the seam allowances toward the top edge of the quilt.

Piecing the Borders

Although it isn't immediately apparent, this quilt contains a narrow outer border composed entirely of triangle-pieced squares. This pieced border completes the overall block pattern at the edges of the quilt top.

1. In the same manner as for the blocks, sew a light A triangle to a dark A triangle and press the seam allowance toward the darker fabric. Make a total of 28 light/dark triangle-pieced squares.

2. Sew a light A triangle to a medium A triangle. Make a total of 56 light/medium triangle-pieced squares.

3. Sew a medium A triangle to a dark A triangle. Make a total of 32 medium/dark triangle-pieced squares.

4. Referring to the **Border Unit Diagram** for placement of color values, sew together eight triangle-pieced squares, forming one border unit, as shown. Press the seam allowances toward the bottom edge of the border unit. Make 14 border units.

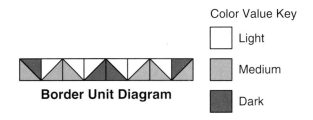

Color Value Key

☐ Light

▨ Medium

■ Dark

Border Unit Diagram

5. Sew four border units together, creating one side border. Press the seam allowances toward the bottom edge of the border. Make one more side border.

6. Referring to the **Quilt Diagram** on page 34, sew the side borders to the left and right sides of the quilt top, pinning carefully to match seams. Press the seam allowances toward the outer edges of the quilt top.

7. Referring to the **Quilt Diagram** for placement of color values, sew three border units together, attaching a medium/dark triangle-pieced square at each end. Make two top and two bottom borders.

8. Referring to the **Quilt Diagram** for placement of color values, sew the top and bottom borders to the top and bottom edges of the quilt top, pinning carefully to match seams. Press the seam allowances toward outer edges of the quilt top.

Quilting and Finishing

1. Mark quilting designs as desired. The quilt shown is quilted by machine, as shown in the **Border Quilting Diagram** and the **Quilting Diagram** on page 34.

Border Quilting Diagram

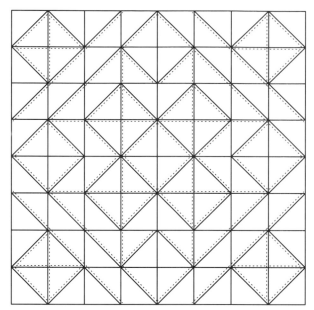

Quilting Diagram

2. Cut the backing fabric into two equal 2⅝-yard lengths. Trim the selvages and divide one piece in half lengthwise. Sew one of these half panels to each side of the full-width panel. Press these seam allowances open. The seams will run parallel to the longer sides of the quilt.

3. Layer the quilt back, batting and quilt top; baste. Trim the quilt back and batting 3 inches larger than the quilt top on all sides.

4. Quilt all marked quilting designs.

5. From the binding fabric, make approximately 310 inches of double-fold, continuous bias binding. See page 164 for instructions on making and attaching binding.

6. Sew the binding to the quilt top. Trim the excess batting and backing. Use matching thread and an invisible stitch to hand finish the binding on the back of the quilt.

Quilt Diagram

Twist and Shout

Quiltmaker: Sue Nickels

Could there be a more ideal project for using up those seemingly "unusable" scraps, snippets, strips, and strings? Sue's freewheeling wall quilt simply swirls with motion, and her brilliant color scheme crackles with excitement. Multicolored floss ties add still another element of fun.

Skill Level: Easy

Size: Finished quilt is 52½ inches square
Finished block is 8½ inches square

Fabrics and Supplies

- ✓ 1½ yards of black striped fabric for the outer border
- ✓ ⅞ yard of black solid fabric for the blocks, appliquéd vine, and binding
- ✓ ¾ yard of white "spotty" print fabric for the borders and corner squares
- ✓ ¼ yard of black multicolored, small-scale floral print for the blocks and corner squares
- ✓ ¼ yard of black "spotty" print fabric for the blocks
- ✓ ¼ yard of bright fuchsia print fabric for the narrow border
- ✓ One 3-inch-square scrap of bright orange check fabric for the corner squares
- ✓ Scraps *totaling* approximately 1½ yards in a wide variety of colors, values, and textures for the leaves, string-pieced blocks, and borders. You'll need lots and lots of bits and pieces, strips and strings, but not much of any single fabric.
- ✓ 3¼ yards of fabric for the quilt back
- ✓ Twin-size batting (72 × 90 inches)
- ✓ Rotary cutter, ruler, and mat
- ✓ Template material
- ✓ Freezer paper
- ✓ A few yards each of orange, bright yellow, fuchsia, and purple embroidery floss
- ✓ A large-eyed, sharp needle

Cutting

Make templates for the leaf appliqué patterns Leaf 1 through Leaf 4 on page 41. Appliqué pattern pieces are finished size; add the seam allowances when cutting them out of the fabric. Instructions for the string-pieced squares and borders are written for using freezer paper foundations. Measurements for the borders are longer than needed; trim them to the exact length when they are added to the quilt top. Cut pieces in the following sequence:

From the black striped fabric, cut:
- Four 5½ × 54-inch strips for the outer borders

From the black solid fabric, cut:
- One 24-inch square for the continuous strip bias binding
- One 18-inch square for the bias vine
- Four 5⅛-inch squares. Cut each square in half diagonally to make 8 A triangles.

From the white spotty print, cut:
- Four 5½ × 27-inch strips for the borders
- Four 5½-inch B corner squares

From the black multicolored print, cut:
- One 5⅛ × 42-inch strip. Cut this strip into six 5⅛-inch squares; cut these squares in half diagonally to make 12 A triangles.
- Four 3-inch C corner squares

From the black spotty fabric, cut:
- One 5⅛ × 42-inch strip. Cut this strip into eight 5⅛-inch squares; cut these squares in half diagonally to make 16 A triangles.

From the fuchsia print, cut:
- Four 1½ × 42-inch strips for the inner borders

From the scrap of orange plaid fabric, cut:
- Four 1½-inch D corner squares

From the wide assortment of scraps in your scrap bag, cut:
- A *total* of 113 leaf appliqués, cutting a random number of pieces from templates Leaf 1 through Leaf 4

Tip: *Leftover scraps from all of the print fabrics can be used for the appliquéd leaves and string-pieced squares and borders. Although some of the leaves may need to be cut from larger scraps, even the tiniest pieces of fabric will work well for string piecing the blocks and borders.*★

Making the String-Pieced Squares

String piecing is a technique by which you actually create your own fabric. Then it's easy to trim it to the exact size you need for your quilt. Using freezer paper as a foundation makes it simple to work with scraps—even tiny "strings" of fabric. And cutting the blocks and borders to the correct sizes later is quick and easy with a rotary cutter and ruler. No real color planning is necessary, either—just reach into your scrap bag and work in random order with whatever you have on hand.

1. Using a rotary cutter and ruler, cut two 3½ × 65-inch freezer paper foundations. These paper foundations will later be cut into 36 string-pieced blocks.

2. Position two strips or scraps of fabric right sides together on the matte side of one of the freezer paper foundations, as shown in **Diagram 1.** Using a ¼-inch seam allowance, sew the fabrics together through the freezer paper foundation, as shown. Open up the seam and finger press the seam flat.

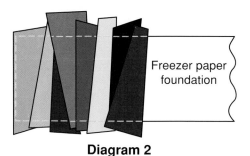

Diagram 1

3. Continue adding scraps of fabric to the freezer paper foundation, as shown in **Diagram 2,** finger pressing each seam flat before adding another piece of fabric. Take advantage of varying widths and angles of your own scraps for an interesting, free-form look. If your scraps are especially large or wide, you may wish to trim them down a bit, to include a wide variety of fabrics in your squares. Take care to cover the entire width and length of the freezer paper foundation as you work, to avoid gaps. Repeat Steps 1 through 3 to string piece another 3½ × 65-inch freezer paper foundation with fabric scraps.

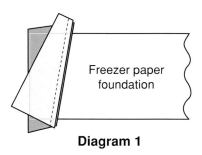

Diagram 2

4. Trim the edges of the fabric scraps even with the edges of the 3½-inch-wide freezer paper foundation, as shown in **Diagram 3.**

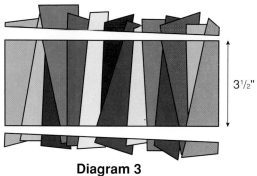

3½"

Diagram 3

5. Using a rotary cutter, cut this strip into 36 string-pieced 3½-inch squares and remove the freezer paper foundation from the wrong side of each square.

REMOVING THE FREEZER PAPER

To remove the freezer paper from the wrong side of the string-pieced squares and borders in this quilt, try this technique. Working from the freezer paper side, simply pinch each seam allowance between your thumb and index finger with the same kind of motion you'd use to separate one postage stamp from another. This helps to separate the freezer paper from the seams and makes it much easier to insert your thumbnail (or the blunt end of a seam ripper) and peel the freezer paper right out. ◆

Making the String-Pieced Borders

1. Using a rotary cutter and ruler, cut four 3 × 38-inch freezer paper foundations.

2. Following the string-piecing procedure as described for the string-pieced squares, cover each of these foundations with fabric scraps.

3. In the same manner, use a rotary cutter to trim the fabrics even with the edges of the 3-inch-wide freezer paper foundations.

Piecing the Blocks

This quilt is composed of nine blocks, each containing four string-pieced squares and four A triangles. The blocks are identical, except for the color placement of the A triangles. Refer to the **Block Diagram** while piecing each block.

1. Sew two string-pieced squares together, pressing the seam allowances in opposite directions. Repeat for the other two squares, as shown in **Diagram 4.**

2. Sew the pairs of squares together, matching the center seam and pressing the seam allowance to one side. Make nine of these string-pieced squares, as shown in **Diagram 5.**

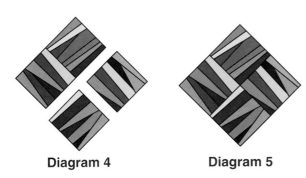

Diagram 4   **Diagram 5**

3. For Block Combination 1, sew a black solid A triangle to opposite edges of the string-pieced unit, as shown in **Diagram 6.** Press the seam allowances toward the A triangles. Complete the block by sewing a black solid A triangle to the remaining two edges. Press the seam allowances toward the A triangles. Make one block in this combination.

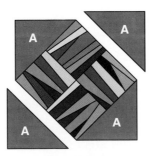

Diagram 6

4. For Block Combination 2, refer to the **Block Diagram** and follow the same procedure, substituting a black spotty A triangle for each black solid A. Make four blocks in this combination.

5. For Block Combination 3, refer to the **Block Diagram** and follow the same piecing procedure, substituting three black floral A triangles and one black solid A triangle to complete the block. Make four blocks in this combination.

Block Combination 1
Make 1

Block Combination 2
Make 4

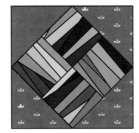

Block Combination 3
Make 4

Block Diagram

Assembling the Quilt Top

1. Referring to the **Quilt Diagram** for block placement, lay out the nine blocks in three rows of three blocks each.

2. Sew the nine blocks together in rows of three blocks each, pressing the seam allowances in opposite directions between the rows.

3. Sew the three rows of blocks together, pressing the seam allowances toward the top edge of the quilt top.

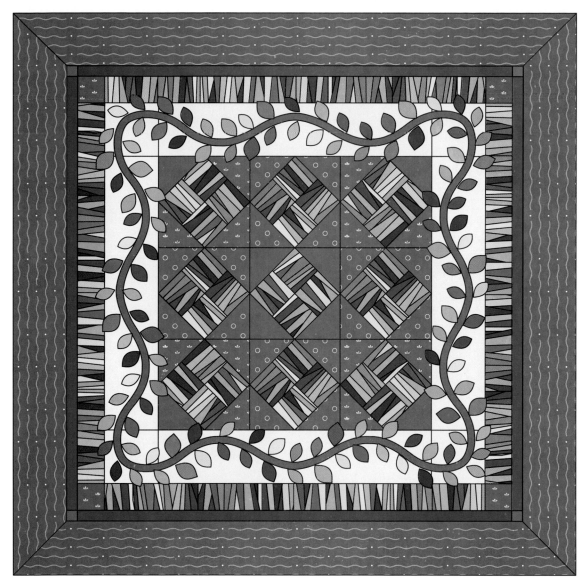

Quilt Diagram

Preparing the Appliqué Vines and Leaves

The quilt shown is appliquéd completely by machine; choose the method of appliqué you prefer.

1. For instructions on making continuous bias, refer to page 165. Use the 18-inch square of black solid fabric to cut a 144-inch continuous bias strip approximately 1⅜ inches wide. Refer to page 158 for tips on using bias presser bars to make perfectly finished vines. Finish the 144-inch-long bias vine to a width of approximately ½ inch.

2. If you choose hand appliqué, refer to page 157 for more information. Prepare the 113 leaf appliqués according to whatever appliqué method you choose.

Adding and Appliquéing the Borders

1. Measure the quilt top both vertically and horizontally. Because the quilt is square, these measurements should be the same. Trim each of the 5½ × 27-inch white spotty print border strips to this measurement.

2. Referring to the **Quilt Diagram** on page 39, sew a trimmed white spotty border strip to the left and right sides of the quilt top. Press the seam allowances toward the border strips.

3. Sew a white spotty B square to each end of the remaining two trimmed border strips. Press the seam allowances away from the B squares. Sew one of these strips to the top and one to the bottom edges of the quilt top, referring to the **Quilt Diagram.** Press the seam allowances toward the border strips.

4. Position the bias vine on the white border, as shown in the **Quilt Diagram.** The vine will be slightly longer than needed; trim it as necessary. Pin or baste the vine in place and stitch it down, using your preferred method of appliqué.

5. Measure the quilt top again and trim each of the string-pieced border strips to this new measurement.

6. Sew a trimmed string-pieced border strip to the left and the right sides of the quilt top. Press the seam allowances away from the string-pieced borders.

7. Sew a black print C square to each end of the remaining two string-pieced border strips. Press the seam allowances toward the C squares. Sew one of these strips to the top and one to the bottom edge of the quilt top, as shown in the **Quilt Diagram.** Press the seam allowances away from the string-pieced border strips.

8. Position the leaf appliqués along the vine, referring to the **Quilt Diagram.** Place approximately 28 leaves on each side, varying their sizes and allowing some of the leaves to overlap the quilt top and the string-pieced borders. Pin or baste each leaf in position and stitch with your preferred method of appliqué.

9. Measure the quilt top with the string-pieced border added and trim the $1\frac{1}{2} \times 42$-inch fuchsia border strips to this new measurement.

10. Sew a trimmed fuchsia border strip to the left and the right sides of the quilt top. Press the seam allowances toward the fuchsia border strips.

11. Sew an orange D corner square to each end of the remaining two fuchsia border strips and press the seam allowances toward the D squares. Sew one of these strips to the top and one to the bottom edge of the quilt top, as shown in the **Quilt Diagram** on page 39. Press the seam allowances toward the fucshia border strips.

12. Sew a $5\frac{1}{2} \times 54$-inch black striped border strip to each side of the quilt top, mitering the corner seams. Refer to page 160 for instructions on mitering seams.

Quilting and Finishing

1. Mark quilting designs as desired. The quilt shown is quilted in the ditch around all of the string-pieced squares, around the appliquéd vines and leaves, and in the ditch between each of the border strips. The A triangles are quilted with free-form feathered vines. The outer black borders are also quilted with feathered vines, as indicated in the **Border Quilting Diagram.** If you wish to do the same type of quilting in the outer borders of your quilt, start by marking a vine that flows in the curves you desire. Use the Feather Motif to mark feathered shapes along the vines. To space the feathers evenly, work from the outer corners inward, so that any necessary adjustments can be made gradually as you approach the center of each border. If you wish to quilt free-form feathered vines in the A triangles, follow the same process for creating curved vines and adding feathered shapes in those areas.

Border Quilting Diagram

2. Divide the backing fabric into two equal $58\frac{1}{2}$-inch pieces. Remove the selvages and sew the pieces together along the long edges. This seam will run parallel to the sides of the quilt. Press the seam allowances open.

3. Layer the quilt back, batting, and quilt top. Position the quilt back so that seam is centered under the quilt top. Baste; then trim the quilt back and batting so that they are approximately 3 inches larger than the quilt top on all sides.

4. Quilt all marked designs, adding additional quilting as desired. The quilt shown was quilted entirely by machine; you may choose to quilt by hand or machine.

5. From the 24-inch-square of black fabric, make approximately 220 inches of double-fold, continuous bias binding. Refer to page 164 for instructions on making and attaching binding.

6. Sew the binding to the quilt top. Trim the excess backing and batting, and use matching thread and an invisible stitch to hand finish the binding on the back side of the quilt.

7. Thread a large-eyed, sharp needle with two strands each of yellow, orange, fuchsia and purple embroidery floss. From the front side of the quilt, insert the threaded needle into the center of each block, referring to the **Quilt Diagram** on page 39. Leave a tail of approximately 3 inches and bring the needle back up to the top of the quilt. Trim the floss even with the first 3-inch tail. Tie the two tails in a square knot and trim the ends to approximately 1 inch. Repeat the process three times in each of the string-pieced borders.

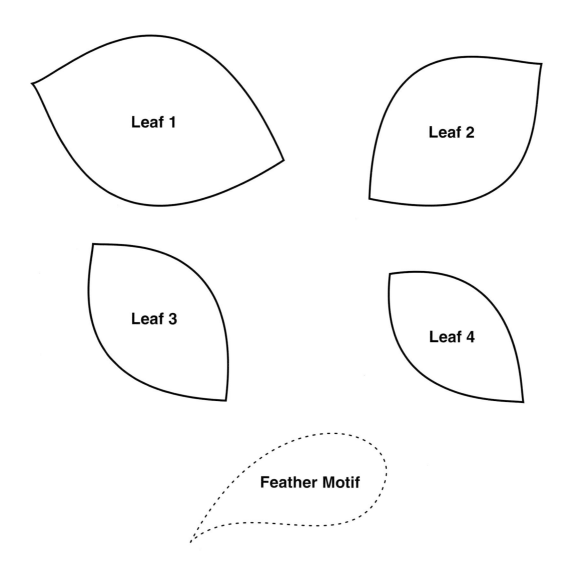

Leaf 1

Leaf 2

Leaf 3

Leaf 4

Feather Motif

Grandmother's Choice

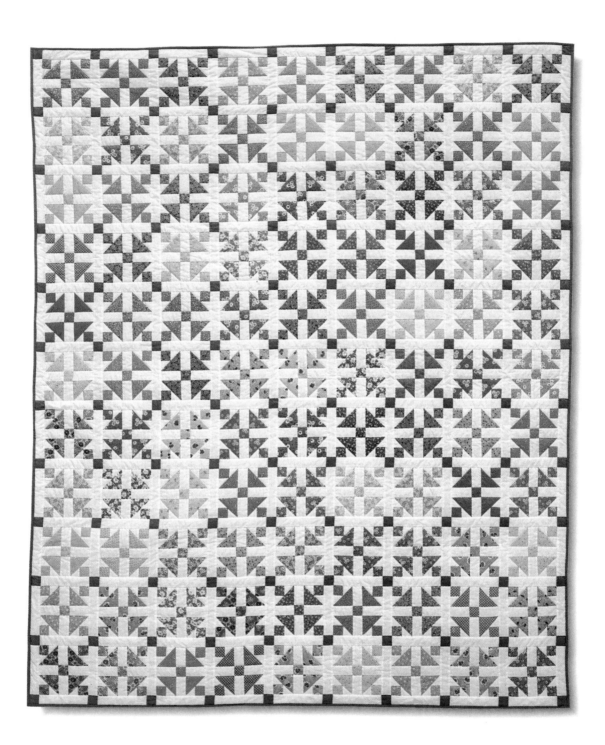

Quiltmaker: Barbara Garrett

Simple elegance and an antique look add to the charm of Barbara's quilt. Her choice of reproduction era prints combined with a complementary "thirties" green re-create the classic look of the beautiful quilts made during that period.

Skill Level: Easy

Size: Finished quilt is 68¾ × 83¾ inches
Finished block is 6¼ inches square

Fabrics and Supplies

Yardages indicate the totals needed of each color and allow for experimenting with your own color arrangements. For example, if ⅞ yard of blue print fabric is listed, you may elect to use ¼ yard *each* of three different blue prints.

✓ 7 yards of white solid fabric for the blocks and sashing strips

✓ 1¾ yards of green solid fabric for corner squares, the blocks, and binding

✓ ⅞ yard of blue print fabrics for the blocks

✓ ⅞ yard of green print fabrics for the blocks

✓ ¾ yard of lavender print fabrics for the blocks

✓ ¾ yard of yellow print fabrics for the blocks

✓ ¾ yard of red print fabrics for the blocks

✓ ½ yard of peach print fabrics for the blocks

✓ 5 yards of fabric for the quilt back

✓ Twin-size batting (72 × 90 inches)

✓ Rotary cutter, ruler, and cutting mat

Cutting

Instructions are for quick-cutting all pieces with a rotary cutter, ruler, and mat. These measurements include ¼-inch seam allowances. Note that quick cutting may result in leftovers.

From the white solid fabric, cut:
- Ten 6¾ × 44-inch strips. Cut these strips into 1¾ × 6¾-inch sashing strips. You will need a total of 218 sashing strips.
- Twenty 2⅛ × 44-inch strips. Cut these strips into three hundred ninety-six 2⅛-inch squares; cut these squares in half diagonally to make 792 B triangles.
- Twenty-nine 1¾ × 44-inch strips. Cut these strips into 1¾ × 3-inch D rectangles. You will need a total of 396 D rectangles.

From the solid green fabric, cut:
- Five 1¾ × 44-inch strips. Cut these strips into 1¾-inch corner squares. You will need a total of 120 corner squares.
- Set the remaining green fabric aside for the binding.

From the lavender print fabrics, cut:
- Four 1¾ × 44-inch strips. Cut these strips into 1¾-inch A squares. You will need a total of 85 A squares.
- Three 3⅜ × 44-inch strips. Cut these strips into thirty-four 3⅜-inch squares; cut these squares in half diagonally to make 68 C triangles

From the blue print fabrics, cut:
- Five 1¾ × 44-inch strips. Cut these strips into 1¾-inch A squares. You will need a total of 105 A squares.
- Four 3⅜ × 44-inch strips. Cut these strips into forty-two 3⅜-inch squares; cut these squares in half diagonally to make 84 C triangles.

From the yellow print fabrics, cut:
- Four 1¾ × 44-inch strips. Cut these strips into 1¾-inch A squares. You will need a total of 75 A squares.
- Three 3⅜ × 44-inch strips. Cut these strips into thirty 3⅜-inch squares; cut these squares in half diagonally to make 60 C triangles

From the green print fabrics, cut:
- Five 1¾ × 44-inch strips. Cut these strips into 1¾-inch A squares. You will need a total of 100 A squares.
- Four 3⅜ × 44-inch strips. Cut these strips into forty 3⅜-inch squares; cut these squares in half diagonally to make 80 C triangles.

From the red print fabrics, cut:
- Four 1¾ × 44-inch strips. Cut these strips into 1¾-inch A squares. You will need a total of 80 A squares.
- Three 3⅜ × 44-inch strips. Cut these strips into thirty-two 3⅜-inch squares; cut these squares in half diagonally to make 64 C triangles.

From the peach print fabrics, cut:
- Three 1¾ × 44-inch strips. Cut these strips into 1¾-inch A squares. You will need a total of 50 A squares.
- Two 3⅜ × 44-inch strips. Cut these strips into twenty 3⅜-inch squares; cut these squares in half diagonally to make 40 C triangles.

Piecing the Blocks

This quilt contains 99 blocks. Of these, 17 blocks are made from lavender prints, 21 from blue prints, 15 from yellow prints, 20 from green prints, 16 from red prints, and 10 from peach prints. Piece each block in the same manner as described here. To duplicate the look of the quilt shown, use the same print fabric within an individual block.

1. Sew two white solid B triangles to a print A square, as shown in **Diagram 1.** Make four of these A/B units.

2. Sew a print C triangle to the A/B unit, as shown in **Diagram 2.** Make four A/B/C units.

Diagram 1　　　**Diagram 2**

3. Sew an A/B/C unit to each side of a white D rectangle, as shown in **Diagram 3.** Repeat to make another segment like this. Press the seam allowances toward the white D rectangles.

Diagram 3

4. Sew two white D rectangles to opposite sides of a print A square, as shown in **Diagram 4.** Press the seam allowances toward the white D rectangles.

| D | A | D |

Diagram 4

5. Sew the three segments of the block together, as shown in the **Block Diagram.** Press the seam allowances toward the white D rectangles.

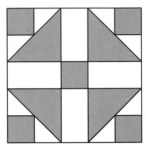

Block Diagram

Assembling the Quilt Top

1. Lay out the quilt blocks and sashing strips in 11 horizontal rows of nine blocks each, according to the color placement you prefer, using the photograph on page 42 as a reference guide.

2. Sew together a row of nine quilt blocks with sashing strips between them and at the beginning and end of the row, as shown in **Diagram 5.** Press the seams toward the white sashing strips. Make 11 of these rows.

3. Sew together a row of nine white sashing strips and 10 green solid corner squares, as shown in **Diagram 6.** Press the seams toward the white sashing strips. Make 12 of these rows.

4. Referring to the **Quilt Diagram,** sew the rows of blocks and rows of sashing strips together. Press the seam allowances toward the sashing strips.

Sashing strip

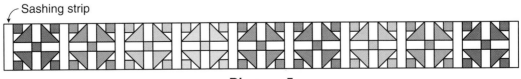

Diagram 5

Diagram 6

BETTER PRESSING

Keep the A square points sharp in each block by sewing two B triangles to a print A square and pressing the seams toward the B triangles, as shown. That way, you'll be able to see the juncture of the two seams while you are adding a print C triangle, making it easy to avoid sewing too far into the seam allowance and "cutting off" the point of the A square. ◆

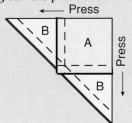

Quilting and Finishing

1. Cut the backing fabric into two pieces that measure 40 × 90 inches and sew them together along the long edges. Press this seam open.

2. Layer the quilt back, batting, and quilt top. Position the quilt backing so that seam is centered under the quilt top; baste. Trim the quilt back and batting to approximately 3 inches larger than the quilt top on all sides.

3. Mark quilting designs as desired. The quilt shown is quilted in the ditch of all of the seams in each block.

4. From the green solid fabric, make approximately 320 inches of double-fold binding. Sew the binding to the quilt top. Trim the excess batting and backing and sew the binding on the back of the quilt by hand. See page 164 for instructions on making and attaching binding.

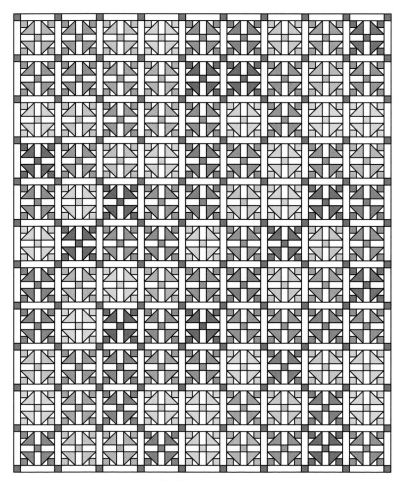

Quilt Diagram

Yellow Monday

Quiltmaker: Elsie Moser

New York Beauty never looked so new! Splashy florals, traditional calicoes, and softly shaded hand-dyed fabrics combine in
this spirited twist on a well-loved favorite. A lavishly appliquéd
border adds the crowning touch to Elsie's arrestingly beautiful
paper-pieced quilt.

Skill Level: Challenging

Size: Finished quilt is 75 inches square
Finished block is 15¼ inches square

Fabrics and Supplies

✓ 2 yards of yellow/purple large-scale floral print fabric for the blocks and borders

✓ 1¾ yards of dusty green print fabric for the blocks and borders

✓ 1⅛ yards of purple tone-on-tone striped fabric for the sashing and border strips

✓ ⅞ yard of olive green solid fabric for the vines and stems

✓ ⅞ yard of gold print fabric for the binding

✓ ¼ yard of fuchsia solid fabric for the corner squares in the blocks and borders

✓ Approximately 4 yards *total* of assorted purple, green, yellow, and gold print, hand-dyed and/or solid scraps for the blocks; each scrap should be 3 inches square, or larger

✓ Approximately 1 yard *total* of assorted purple and fuchsia scraps for the blocks and grape appliqués. Hand-dyed fabrics work beautifully, as do solids, and subtly textured, tone-on-tone prints.

✓ Approximately ½ yard total of assorted olive green print scraps for the leaf appliqués

✓ 4½ yards of fabric for the quilt back

✓ Full-size quilt batting (80 × 96 inches)

✓ Rotary cutter, ruler, and mat

✓ Template material

✓ Tracing paper or freezer paper for paper piecing

✓ Thread to match appliqué pieces

Cutting

The patterns for the leaf and grape appliqués on pages 54–56 do not require seam allowances. Add seam allowances as you cut each piece from fabric. Instructions are given for quick cutting the corner squares; sashing and border strips; and the A, B, and C strips with a rotary cutter and ruler. All of these measurements include ¼-inch seam allowances. Be aware that quick-cutting methods sometimes result in leftover pieces. Measurements for the borders are slightly longer than needed; trim them to the appropriate length when they are added to the quilt top.

Cut pieces in the following sequence:

From the yellow/purple floral, cut:
• Four 4¼ × 63-inch border strips
• 64 E pieces
• 4 J pieces

From the dusty green, cut:
• Four 2½ × 63-inch border strips
• 4 K pieces. The remaining fabric may be included in the green scrap fabric used for the blocks.

From the purple stripe, cut:
• Six 1¾ × 44-inch strips. Cut these strips into 1¾ × 14½-inch L strips. You will need a total of 12 L strips.
• Fourteen 1¾ × 44-inch strips. Cut these strips into 1¾ × 7½-inch G strips. You will need a total of 72 G strips; use leftovers from the previous step if necessary.

From the olive green solid, cut:
• One 30-inch square to be used for making continuous bias strips for the vines and stems

From the ¼ yard of fuchsia solid, cut:
• Two 1¾ × 44-inch strips. Cut these strips into 1¾-inch H corner squares. You will need a total of 32 H corner squares.
• 4 I pieces. The balance of this fabric can be used for grape appliqués.

From the assorted purple, green, yellow and gold scraps, cut:
• Three hundred eighty-four 1¾ × 3-inch A strips. Cut in sets of six strips, each from the same color but not necessarily the same fabric, for a total of 64 sets of six A strips each. "Look-alike" fabrics may be substituted if you run short of a specific fabric to complete a set.
• Three hundred twenty 2 × 3-inch B strips. Cut in sets of five strips, each from the same fabric, for a total of 64 sets of five B strips each.
• One hundred twenty-eight 1½ × 3-inch C strips. Cut two strips that match each set of B strips.

- 64 F pieces
- 64 F reverse pieces. These do not need to match the F pieces.
- 64 D pieces. Cut these from the purple and green scraps only.

From the assorted purple and fuchsia scraps, cut:
- 300 grapes, using the grape templates on page 56. You may cut equal numbers (75) of each size or any combination of sizes you like.

From the assorted olive green prints, cut:
- 19 small leaf appliqués
- 16 large leaf appliqués

Making the Paper Foundations

The pieced curved arc portions shown in the **Unit Diagram** are paper pieced. The remainder of these units are sewn without paper foundations. The finished blocks contain four of these units, for a total of 64 units and 16 finished blocks.

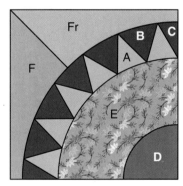

Unit Diagram

1. Make eight photocopies of the Paper Piecing Foundation Pattern on page 54. Be sure they are 100 percent accurate in size.

2. Layer eight sheets of tracing or freezer paper underneath one of the photocopied Paper Piecing Foundation Patterns and staple the edges together to hold them in place. Repeat this process for each of the remaining photocopies.

3. Using a short-to-medium stitch length and no thread on top or in the bobbin of the sewing machine, stitch over the seam lines of the pieced arc as shown in **Diagram 1.** These needlepunched lines in the paper will become your sewing lines as you add fabric to the foundations. Working through the photocopy and the layers of tracing paper at the same time, cut out the foundation patterns along the solid lines.

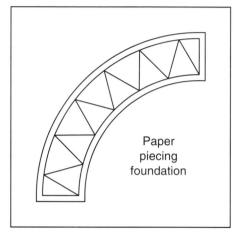

Diagram 1

Paper Piecing the Curved Arcs

For each unit, all A triangles should be from one or more similar fabrics in the same color family. All B and C triangles should be from a single fabric that contrasts strongly in color and/or value to the A pieces. Lay out several A, B, and C strips in various color combinations before sewing each pieced arc together. This will allow you to establish a balance of color and an effective contrast of value within the units.

1. Layer an A strip on top of a C strip, right sides together and position these strips underneath one of the paper piecing foundations, so that the C strip lies against the paper foundation, as shown in **Diagram 2.** The edges of the A and C strips must extend ¼ inch beyond the first seam line on the paper foundation, as shown. Starting and ending at the edges of the A and C strips, sew the first seam line (see the numbered seam line on the Paper Piecing Foundation Pattern for reference). Open up the A and C strips and press the seam flat.

2. Referring to **Diagram 3,** trim the edges of the opened A and C strips to ¼ inch beyond the second seam line.

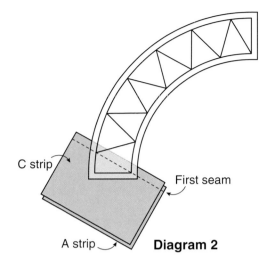

Diagram 2

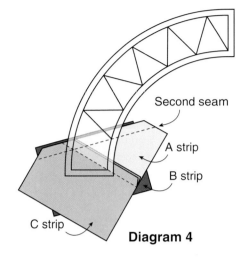

Diagram 4

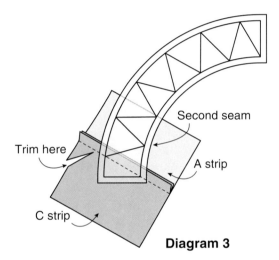

Diagram 3

3. Referring to **Diagram 4,** place a B strip right sides together with the A and C strips, matching the raw edges, as shown. Sew this second seam, open it up and press it flat. Trim the B strip to ¼ inch beyond the next seam.

4. In the same manner, continue sewing A and B strips in the numbered sequence shown on the Paper Piecing Foundation Pattern until there are five A strips, six B strips, and a final C strip on the tracing paper foundation. Press each seam flat as you go. This completes one pieced arc, as shown in the **Unit Diagram.**

5. Trim the edges of all A, B, and C strips even with the curved edges and the ends of the tracing paper foundation. Do not remove the tracing paper foundation at this time.

6. Repeat Steps 1 through 5 to make a total of 64 pieced arcs.

Piecing the Blocks

The F and F reverse pieces should be of two different, contrasting fabrics.

1. Sew a D piece to an E piece as shown in **Diagram 5,** taking care to match midpoint markings and pin generously. For more information on piecing curved seams, see page 59.

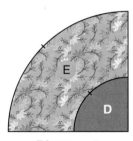

Diagram 5

2. Sew the combined D/E unit to the completed arc of A/B/C triangles, matching midpoints, as shown in **Diagram 6.**

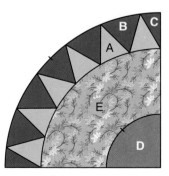

Diagram 6

3. Sew an F piece to an F reverse piece, as shown in **Diagram 7.**

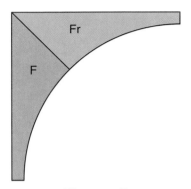

Diagram 7

4. Sew the F/F reverse unit to remaining portion of the unit, as shown in the **Unit Diagram** on page 48. As for any curved seam, take care to match midpoints and pin generously before sewing.

5. Repeat Steps 1 through 4 to make a total of 64 units.

Assembling the Blocks

Each block is composed of four pieced units, four G strips, and one H square. Refer to the **Block Diagram** and the photograph on page 46 for color guidance, and sew each block in the following sequence.

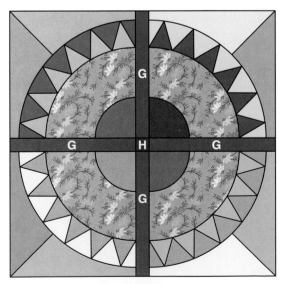

Block Diagram

1. Referring to the **Block Diagram,** sew one pieced unit to each side of a G strip. Press the seam allowances toward the G strip. Make two of these rows.

2. Referring to the **Block Diagram,** sew a G strip to each side of an H square and press the seam allowances toward the G strips.

3. Referring to the **Block Diagram,** sew the three parts of the block together, matching seams carefully. Since the seam allowances have been pressed in opposite directions, they should "nest" together well. Press the seam allowances toward the center G/H/G strip.

4. Make a total of 16 blocks.

Assembling the Quilt Top

1. Referring to the **Quilt Diagram,** lay out the 16 completed blocks in four rows of four blocks each. Arrange the blocks in the color balance that pleases you.

2. Referring to the **Quilt Diagram,** sew the blocks into four horizontal rows, pressing the seams allowances between blocks in opposite directions from row to row.

3. Referring to the **Quilt Diagram,** sew the four rows of blocks together, matching seams carefully. Press the seam allowances toward the top edge of the quilt top.

4. Use your thumbnail or the blunt end of a seam ripper to carefully remove the tracing paper foundations from the curved pieced arcs in each block.

Assembling the Borders

1. Sew a G strip to an H square, as shown in **Diagram 8.** Press the seam allowances away from the H square. Make eight G/H units.

Diagram 8

2. Sew together one L strip, an H square, an L strip, an H square, and another L strip, as shown in **Diagram 9.** Press all seam allowances away from the H squares. Make four L/H strips.

Quilt Diagram

3. Sew a short G/H strip to each end of the four long L/H strips, as shown in **Diagram 10.** Press the seam allowances away from the H squares, completing the four pieced border strips.

4. Crease the midpoint of one of the pieced border strips. Then crease the midpoint of one yellow/purple floral border strip and one dusty green border strip. Matching the midpoints, sew

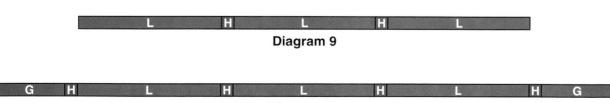

Diagram 9

Diagram 10

together the three border strips, as shown in the **Border Diagram.** Press all seam allowances toward the green border strip. Trim the floral and dusty green borders as necessary. Make four of these border units.

5. Crease the midpoints of the top and bottom edges of the quilt top. Matching midpoints and seams, sew a border unit to the top and bottom edges of the quilt top, referring to the **Quilt Diagram** on page 51. The pieced border lies closest to the center of the quilt top. Press the seam allowances toward the outer edges of the quilt.

6. Sew an I piece to a J piece, as shown in **Diagram 11,** taking care to match marked midpoints and pin generously. Press the seam allowance toward the I piece. Make four I/J units.

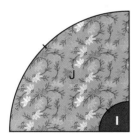

Diagram 11

7. Sew a K piece to an I/J unit, as shown in **Diagram 12,** matching and pinning carefully. Press the seam allowance toward the J piece. Make four of these corner block units.

8. Referring to the **Quilt Diagram,** sew a corner block unit to each end of the remaining two border units. Press the seam allowances toward the border units.

9. Crease the midpoint on both sides of the quilt top. Referring to the **Quilt Diagram,** sew a border unit to each side of the quilt top, matching seams carefully. Press the seam allowances toward the outer edges of the quilt.

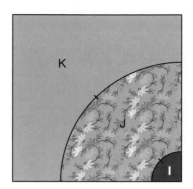

Diagram 12

Appliquéing the Borders

The appliqué borders in this quilt have a charming, free-form quality. There is no exact placement for each leaf or grape. Use your preferred method for preparing the leaves and grapes for appliqué. For more information on hand appliqué, see page 157.

1. Use the 30-inch square of olive green fabric to make a continuous bias strip for the border vines and stems. Cut the continuous bias strip 1⅜ inches wide. Trim off a segment 250 inches (approximately 7 yards) long to use for the vine and set the balance aside to use for the stems. The finished border vine should be approximately ½ inch wide. For more information on continuous bias strips, see page 164.

2. Using the quilt photograph on page 46 as a placement guide, pin the vine to the outer (floral/dusty green) border of the quilt top, trimming excess length if necessary.

3. Place and pin three small and four large leaf appliqués on each border, scattering a few extra leaves to casually overlap the inner borders. Use the remainder of the appliqués for the partial leaves along the edges of the quilt. Refer to the quilt photograph for guidance on leaf placement.

Border Diagram

INVISIBLE STOPS AND STARTS

To make the border vine appear to have no beginning or ending, arrange leaves and vines in a way that will allow you to hide the beginning and the end of the border vine strip underneath them. Once you are satisfied, hand baste the vine in place around the entire border. ◆

4. Trim the remaining continuous bias strip to a width of 1⅛ inches. Use bias bars to prepare a strip that finishes approximately ⅜ inch wide. Cut this strip into 35 stem segments that range from 1½ to 2 inches long. For more information on using bias bars, see page 158.

5. Connect the leaves to the vine by tucking the raw edges of a stem under both the leaf and the vine. Pin or baste the stems in place.

6. Appliqué the vine, leaves, and stems in place using a blind stitch and thread that matches the appliqué pieces. To avoid excess stretching of the bias strips, appliqué the inner curves of the vine first. Do not trim away the fabric behind the appliqué shapes in this quilt.

Tip: *Exception: If you choose the freezer paper appliqué method described on page 157, you'll need to remove the freezer paper.* ★

7. Use the quilt photograph for assistance in placing the grapes along the vine. Grapes may be grouped in large and small bunches, with varying sizes in each bunch. The quilt shown has approximately 76 grapes on the top border, 62 on the right, 89 on the bottom, and 73 on the left border, and no two clusters are exactly alike. Appliqué the grapes using a blind stitch and thread that matches the appliqué pieces.

Quilting and Finishing

1. Mark quilting designs as desired. The quilt shown is quilted in the ditch around pieces A through E, as shown in the **Block Quilting Diagram,** as well as around all sashing and appliqué shapes. The border vine is echo quilted at approximately 2-inch intervals through both the floral and dusty green borders.

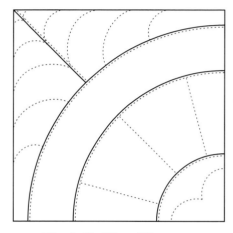

Block Quilting Diagram

2. To piece the quilt back, divide the backing fabric into two 2¼-yard pieces and remove the selvages. Divide one of the 2¼-yard pieces in half lengthwise, and sew each half to the long sides of the remaining full piece. Press the seams away from the center panel. The seams of the quilt back will lie parallel to the sides of the quilt.

3. Layer the quilt back, batting, and quilt top; baste. Trim the quilt back and batting 3 inches larger than the quilt top on all sides.

4. Quilt all marked designs, and add additional quilting if desired.

5. From the binding fabric, make approximately 310 inches of double-fold, continuous bias binding. For details on making and attaching continuous bias binding, see page 164.

6. Sew the binding to the quilt top. Trim the excess batting and backing, and use matching thread and a blind stitch to hand finish the binding on the back of the quilt.

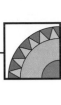

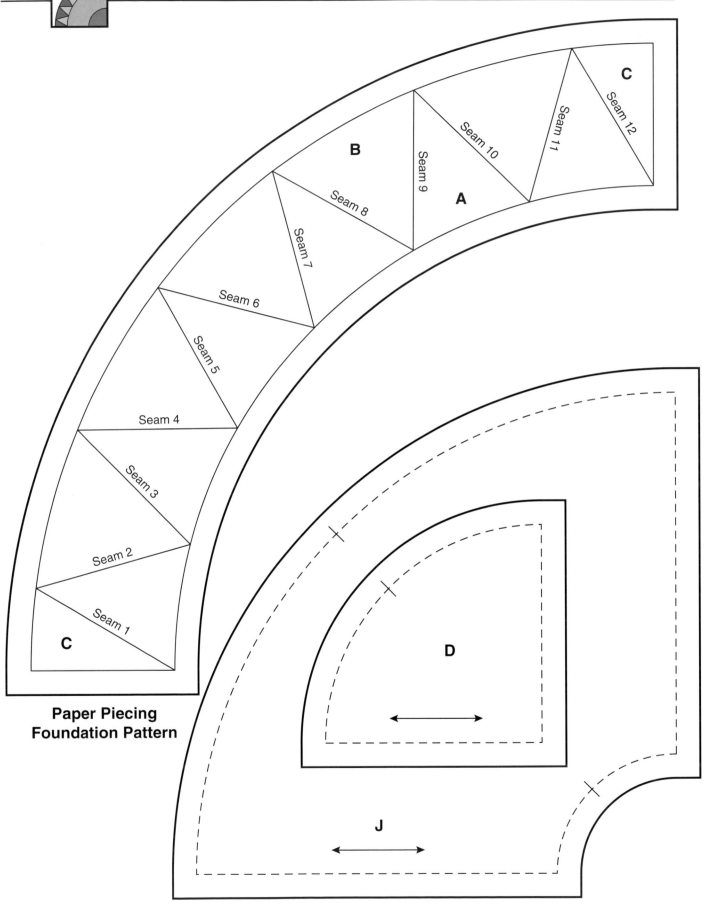

C

Seam 12

Seam 11

Seam 10

Seam 9

A

B

Seam 8

Seam 7

Seam 6

Seam 5

Seam 4

Seam 3

Seam 2

Seam 1

C

**Paper Piecing
Foundation Pattern**

D

J

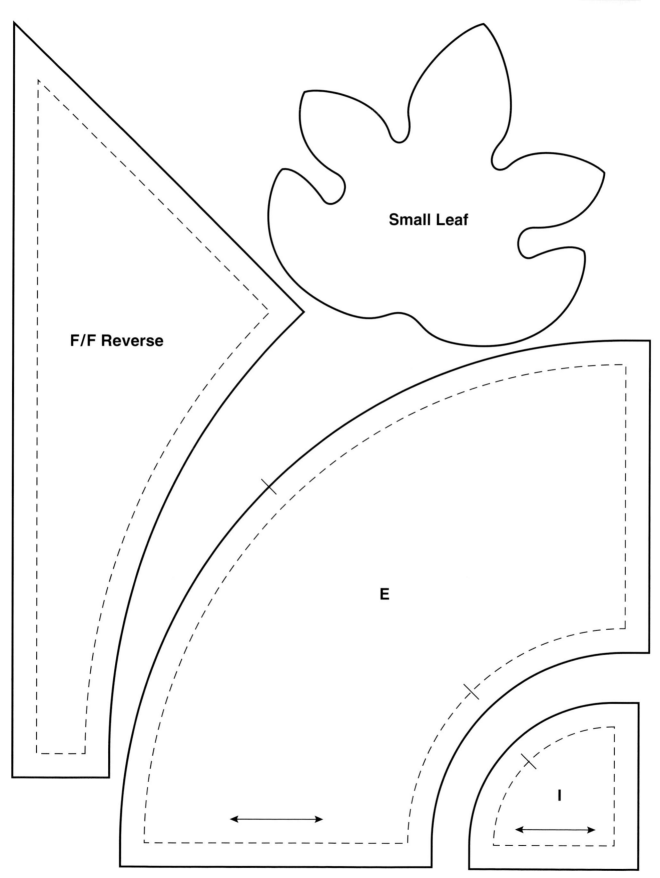

F/F Reverse

Small Leaf

E

I

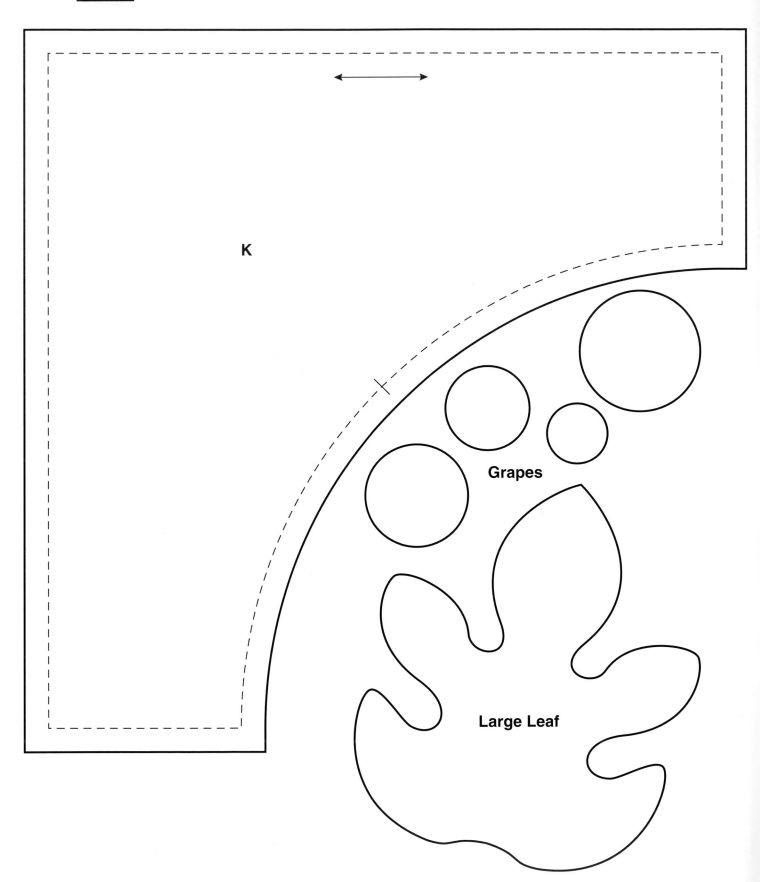

K

Grapes

Large Leaf

Cherry Basket

Quiltmaker: Carol B. Hood

The handwork of a young nineteenth-century Kentucky girl provided the inspiration for this exquisite combination of piecing and appliqué. Carol adapted the design and selected the fabrics—an unusual mix of rust paisley, gold geometric, rose plaid, and navy solid—and her quilt group helped her to realize this modern-day masterpiece. The blocks are stipple-quilted for an exceptionally rich, sculpted look.

Skill Level: Challenging

Size: Finished quilt is 87 × 92 inches
Finished block is 20 inches square

Fabrics and Supplies

- ✓ 6 yards of unbleached muslin for the background squares and borders
- ✓ 2 yards of rich red solid fabric for the cherries, inner border, and binding
- ✓ 2 yards of navy blue solid fabric for the blocks
- ✓ 1 yard of rust paisley fabric for the blocks
- ✓ ⅔ yard of rosy pink plaid fabric for the blocks
- ✓ ⅔ yard of gold print fabric for the blocks
- ✓ 2½ yards of 108-inch-wide unbleached muslin (or 6 yards of 45-inch-wide unbleached muslin) for the quilt back
- ✓ Queen-size batting (90 × 108 inches)
- ✓ Rotary cutter, ruler, and mat
- ✓ Template material
- ✓ One 20½-inch square and one 12½-inch square of tracing paper
- ✓ Black permanent fabric marking pen
- ✓ Water-soluble marker or mechanical pencil
- ✓ Navy embroidery floss
- ✓ Embroidery needle

Cutting

The instructions are for quick cutting the background squares and borders with a rotary cutter and ruler. These measurements include ¼-inch seam allowances. Measurements for the borders are longer than needed; trim them to the length needed when sewing them to the quilt top.

Full-size patterns for all other patchwork and appliqué pieces are shown on pages 64–67. Transfer these patterns to template material. Pattern pieces A through P as well as T, U, and V include ¼-inch seam allowances. To cut pieces A reverse through I reverse, flip each template over to the reverse side before placing it on the fabric.

Because of the complexity of this quilt, you may find it helpful to make two separate stacks of fabric for each piece that needs to be reversed, clearly labeling one of them "reverse pieces."

The appliqué patterns Q, R, and S are shown finished size. Add the seam allowances when cutting each piece out of fabric. For more information on hand appliqué, see page 157. Cut pieces in the following order:

From the muslin, cut:
- Two 17½ × 44-inch strips for the top border
- Three 12½ × 65-inch strips for the side and bottom borders
- Nine 20½-inch background squares for the center blocks
- Two 12½-inch background squares for the corner blocks

From the rich red solid fabric, cut:
- Four 2 × 65-inch strips for the inner border
- One 32-inch square for the bias binding
- 160 S cherries

From the navy solid fabric, cut:
- One 30-inch square for the bias stems and large urn handles
- 9 E and 9 E reverse petals for the large flowers
- 40 I and 40 I reverse petals for the small flowers
- 94 R leaves
- 2 V pieces for the small corner urn tops

From the rust paisley fabric, cut:
- 9 B and 9 B reverse petals for the large flowers
- 9 D and 9 D reverse petals for the large flowers
- 9 K pieces for the large urns
- 9 M pieces for the large urns
- 9 O pieces for the large urns
- 40 H and 40 H reverse petals for the small flowers
- 2 T pieces for the small corner urns

From the rosy pink plaid fabric, cut:
- 9 C and 9 C reverse petals for the large flowers
- 9 L pieces for the large urns
- 9 N pieces for the large urns

- 40 G and 40 G reverse petals for the small flowers
- 2 U pieces for the small corner urns

From the gold print fabric, cut:
- 9 A and 9 A reverse petals for the large flowers
- 9 J pieces for the large urns
- 9 P pieces for the large urns
- 9 Q pieces for the large urn mouths
- 40 F and 40 F reverse petals for the small flowers

Preparing the Appliqué Pieces

There are nine blocks at the center of this quilt, each consisting of one large flower, four small flowers, and a large urn. If you're a fan of hand piecing, this quilt may become one of your all-time favorites, although machine piecers will find it easy to achieve these gently curved seams, too. After the flowers and urns are pieced together, they are then appliquéd onto muslin background squares. The urn handles and mouths are stitched first, followed by stems, leaves, and cherries. Finally, chain stitch stems are embroidered in navy floss, connecting the cherries to the appliquéd stems.

Assembling the Large Flowers

1. Sew a gold A petal to a rust B petal, stopping the line of stitching ¼ inch in from the raw edge at the pointed end of the petals, as indicated by the dot shown in **Diagram 1.** Press the seams allowance toward the B petal.

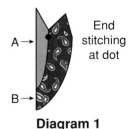

A→ End stitching at dot

B→

Diagram 1

2. In the same manner, sew a rosy print C petal to a rust D petal, and then add a navy solid E petal, as shown in **Diagram 2.** Press the seam allowances toward the E petal.

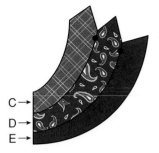

C→
D→
E→

Diagram 2

3. Sew the A/B unit to the C/D/E unit, completing the right half of the large flower, as shown in **Diagram 3.** Press the seam allowance toward the C petal.

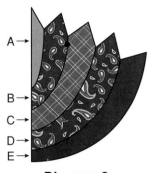

A→

B→

C→

D→

E→

Diagram 3

PIECING CURVED SEAMS

To sew any of the curved seams in this quilt, just follow these easy tricks. Referring to **Diagram 1,** start by creasing the midpoints of both a convex and a concave piece. Make a few clips into the concave seam allowance, so that each clip is approximately ¼ inch apart and about ⅛ inch deep. Then, with the clipped seam allowance on top, place the right sides of the two curved pieces together, matching the beginnings, midpoints, and ends of the two seam allowances. That way, it will be easy to adjust the clipped seam allowance of the concave piece to fit the other piece and sew them together effortlessly. ◆

4. Repeat Steps 1 through 3, using the A reverse through E reverse pieces to create the left half of the large flower, as shown in **Diagram 4.**

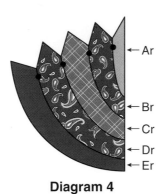

← Ar
← Br
← Cr
← Dr
← Er

Diagram 4

5. Sew the two units together, completing the large flower, as shown in **Diagram 5.** Press the center seam allowance open.

6. Make a total of nine large flowers.

Large Flower
Diagram 5

Assembling the Small Flowers

1. Sew a gold F petal to a rosy pink G petal, stopping the stitching ¼ inch in from the raw edge at the pointed end of the petals, as indicated by the dot in **Diagram 6.** Press the seam allowances toward the G petal.

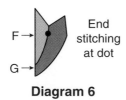

F →

G →

End stitching at dot

Diagram 6

2. In the same manner, sew a rust H petal to a navy solid I petal, as shown in **Diagram 7.** Press the seam allowance toward the I petal.

H →
I →

Diagram 7

3. Sew the F/G and H/I units together, forming the right half of a small flower, as shown in **Diagram 8.** Stop the line of stitching ¼ inch in from the raw edges, as shown, and press the seam allowances toward the H petal.

F →

G →
H →
I →

Diagram 8

4. Repeat Steps 1 through 3, using the F reverse through I reverse petals to create the left half of the small flower, as shown in **Diagram 9.**

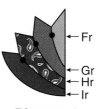

← Fr

← Gr
← Hr
← Ir

Diagram 9

5. Sew the two units together, completing the small flower, as shown in **Diagram 10.** Press the center seam allowance open.

Small Flower
Diagram 10

6. Make 40 small flowers; 4 will be used in each of the nine large center blocks and 2 in each of the small corner blocks.

Assembling the Large Urns

1. Sew the pieces of the large urn in the following order, beginning at the top: a gold J, a rust K, a rosy pink L, a rust M, a rosy pink N, a rust O, and a gold P, as shown in **Diagram 11.** Press all seam allowances toward the J piece. Make a total of nine large urns.

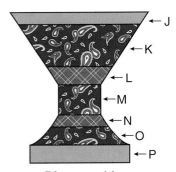

Diagram 11

Assembling the Small Urns

1. Sew the pieces of the small urn in the following order, beginning at the top: a rust T, a rosy pink U, and a navy solid V, as shown in **Diagram 12.** Press the seam allowances toward the V piece. Make a total of two small urns.

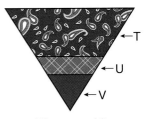

Diagram 12

Preparing the Stems and Urn Handles

1. Use the 30-inch square of navy solid fabric to cut a continuous bias strip approximately ⅞ inch wide. For more information on continuous-cut bias strips, refer to page 165.

This strip will be used to cut the stems and urn handles for the nine center blocks as well as the stems in the two corner blocks. These strips should be approximately ¼ inch wide when finished. Refer to page 158 for how to use bias presser bars for making finished bias stems.

2. Prepare the following for each of the nine center blocks, referring to the **Center Block Diagram:**

- Two 9-inch segments for stem 1
- Three 6½-inch segments for stem 2
- Two 5½-inch segments for stem 3
- Two 4½-inch urn handles

3. Prepare the following for each of the two corner blocks, referring to the **Corner Block Diagram** on page 62:

- Two 6½-inch segments for stem 4
- Two 5½ inch segments for stem 5

Appliquéing the Center Blocks

Each of the nine center blocks requires one gold Q urn mouth, 10 navy solid R leaves, 16 red S cherries, two stem 1s, three stem 2s, two stem 3s, one pieced urn, and one large and four small flowers. Prepare each piece according to your preferred method of hand appliqué.

Embroidered chain stitch stems

Center Block Diagram

1. Make a master pattern for positioning the appliqué pieces on the background squares by folding a 20½-inch square of tracing paper in half vertically, horizontally, and diagonally in both directions. Referring to the **Center Block Diagram** on page 61 for correct placement of the appliqué shapes, use a pencil to draw the outlines of the finished shapes on the tracing paper. Take care to use only the finished appliqué shapes for creating this master pattern and remember that some of the shapes overlap. When you have completed the master pattern, darken your drawn lines with a permanent marking pen and allow the ink to dry before marking appliqué guidelines on the fabric background squares.

2. Fold one of the 20½-inch background squares in half vertically, horizontally, and diagonally both ways, and crease it lightly.

3. Center the background square over the master pattern. Using a water-soluble fabric marker or a mechanical pencil, lightly transfer the guidelines from the master pattern to the background fabric.

4. Place two stem 2s and two urn handles in the correct positions on the marked background square, remembering that the raw edges will be overlapped by the Q urn mouth and the pieced urn. Pin or baste them in place and appliqué with a blind stitch.

5. Pin a gold Q urn mouth in place, carefully positioning and pinning two stem 3s, two stem 1s, and one stem 2 in place, so that they overlap the upper portion and underlap the lower portion of the Q urn mouth, as shown in the **Center Block Diagram.**

6. Appliqué the upper portion of the urn mouth, moving the stems gently out of the way as you work and make sure to cover the raw edges of the stem 2s at each side.

7. Appliqué stems 1, 2 and 3 in place over the upper portion of the Q urn mouth.

8. Appliqué the pieced urn in place, covering the raw edges of the urn handles.

9. Appliqué the lower portion of the urn mouth in place, covering the stems and the top edge of the pieced urn.

10. In the same manner, appliqué the large flower, four small flowers, 10 R leaves, and 16 S

cherries in place, covering the raw edges of the stems.

11. Using three strands of navy embroidery floss and an embroidery needle, connect the berries to the stem 2s with a chain stitch.

12. Make a total of nine center blocks.

Appliquéing the Corner Blocks

1. Prepare a master pattern in the same manner as for the center blocks, using a 12½-inch square of tracing paper. Mark appliqué guidelines on both of the 12½-inch fabric background corner squares, referring to the **Corner Block Diagram** for guidance in placement of the appliqué shapes.

Corner Block Diagram

2. Place two stem 4s and two stem 5s in the correct positions on the marked background square. Pin or baste them in place and appliqué.

3. In the same manner, add one small urn, two small flowers, two R leaves, and eight S cherries.

4. Using three strands of navy embroidery floss, chain stitch stems to connect the cherries to the stem 4s.

5. Make two corner blocks.

Assembling the Quilt Top

1. Referring to the **Quilt Diagram,** sew the nine center blocks into three rows of three blocks each. Press the seam allowances in opposite directions between blocks.

2. Sew the three rows of blocks together, pressing the seam allowances in opposite directions in alternate rows.

3. Sew a 2 × 65-inch red border strip to each of the four sides of the quilt top, mitering the corner seams and trimming the border strips as necessary. For more information on mitering, see page 160.

4. Measure the quilt horizontally through the center of the quilt top. Trim two of the 12½ ×

65-inch border strips to this measurement. Sew these borders to the left and right sides of the quilt and press the seam allowances toward the borders.

5. Measure the quilt vertically through the center of the quilt top. Trim the remaining 12½ × 65-inch border strip to this measurement.

6. Sew a 12½-inch corner block to each end of this 12½-inch-wide border strip and press the seam allowances away from the corner blocks.

Quilt Diagram

7. Sew this border strip to the bottom edge of the quilt top and press the seam allowances toward the edge of the quilt.

8. Sew together the two 17½ × 44-inch border strips and press the seam allowance to one side. Sew this border to the top edge of the quilt top, trimming the strip as necessary. Press the seam allowances toward the edge of the quilt.

Quilting and Finishing

1. Mark all quilting designs as desired. The border of the quilt shown is quilted in an elaborate cable and feather motif, as indicated in the **Border Quilting Diagram.** A 1-inch diagonal grid fills the remainder of the border areas, as shown.

2. If you choose 45-inch wide fabric for your quilt back, cut the 6-yard length of fabric into two 3-yard pieces. Trim the selvage edge from one long side of each piece and sew these edges right sides together with a ¼-inch seam allowance. Press this seam open.

3. Layer the quilt back, batting, and quilt top; baste. Trim the quilt back and batting to approximately 3 inches larger than the quilt top on all sides.

4. Quilt all marked designs. In addition to the border quilting designs, this quilt is also quilted in the ditch around the red borders and around each of the flowers and urns. The background of each block has lines of stipple quilting at approximately ⅛-inch intervals following the outlines of the appliqué shapes and extending to the outer edges of the block.

5. Make approximately 370 inches of double-fold, continuous bias binding from the 32-inch square of red solid fabric. Refer to page 164 for instructions on making and attaching binding.

6. Sew the binding to the quilt top. Trim the excess batting and backing. Use matching thread and an invisible stitch to hand finish the binding on the back of the quilt.

Border Quilting Diagram

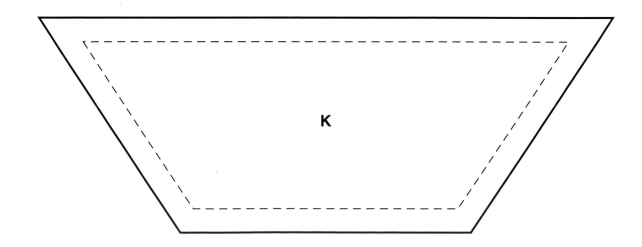

K

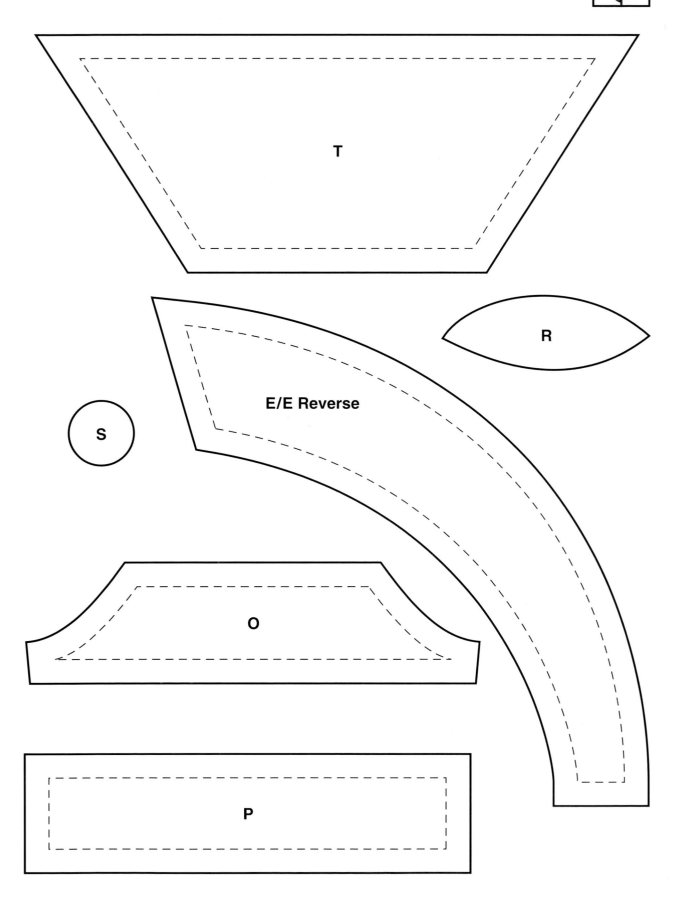

T

R

E/E Reverse

S

O

P

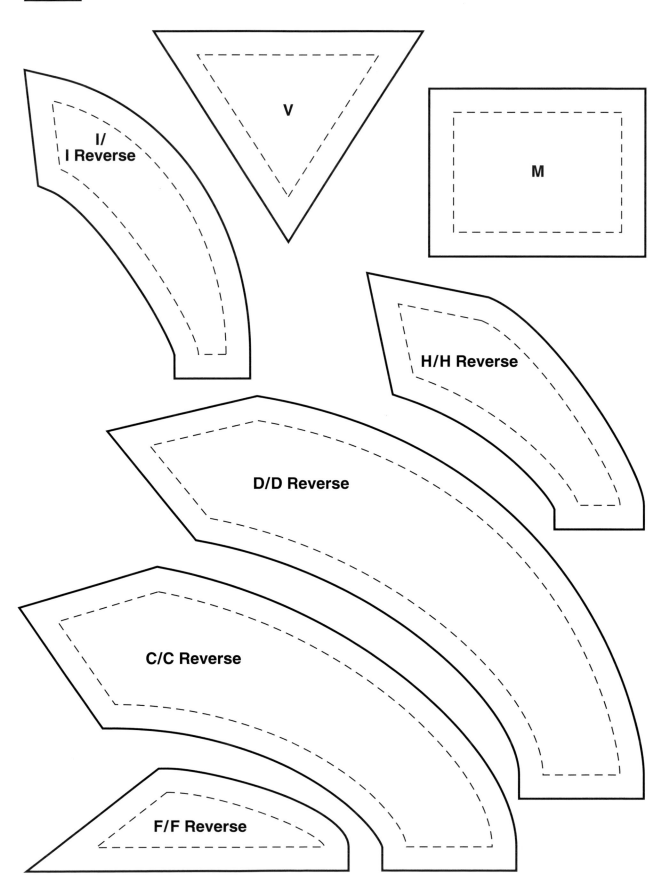

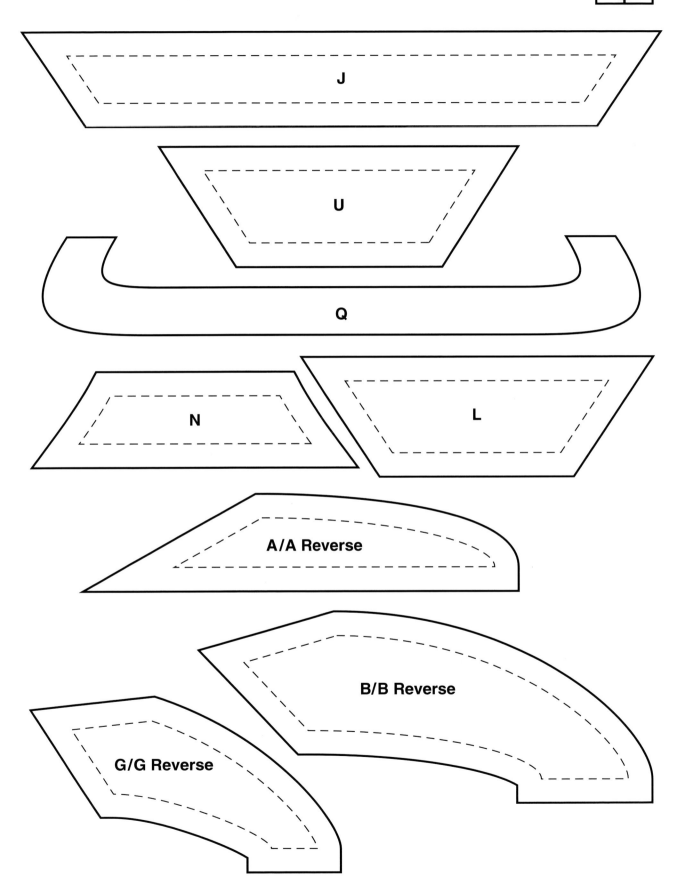

Tessellating Sea Horses

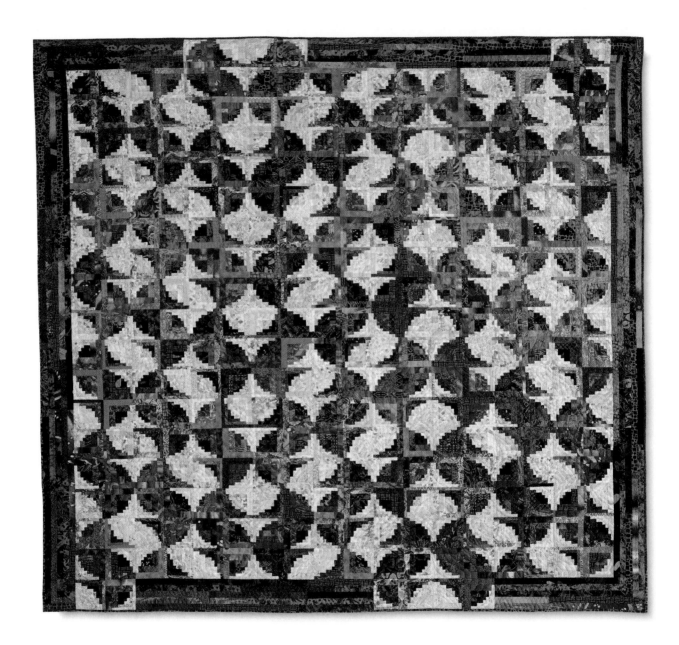

Quiltmaker: Donna Radner

Sea horses frolic through an underwater fantasyland in this clever variation of the familiar Log Cabin. Inspired by *Log Cabin in the Round Designs* by Barbara Schaffeld and Bev Vickery, Donna has created the illusion of curves in her quilt without a single curved seam. Her results are dramatic, yet you'll be surprised at how simple this technique really is.

Skill Level: Intermediate

Size: Finished quilt is 95 × 100 inches
Finished block is 5 inches square

Fabrics and Supplies

While many traditional florals and small-scale prints will mix well with the "underwater" theme of this quilt, combine them with lots of large-scale florals and exotic prints, abstracts, batiks, and other unusual prints, too.

- ✓ Scraps *totaling* approximately 4½ yards of a wide variety of light pink, blue, and teal prints for the blocks
- ✓ Scraps *totaling* approximately 4½ yards of a wide variety of medium and dark blues and teals for the blocks and borders
- ✓ Scraps *totaling* approximately 3½ yards of a wide variety of medium and dark fuchsias and purples for the blocks and borders
- ✓ ½ yard *each* of a dark blue fabric and a teal print fabric for the binding
- ✓ 9 yards of fabric for the quilt back
- ✓ King-size batting (120 inches square)
- ✓ Rotary cutter, ruler, and mat

Cutting

Instructions are for quick cutting the blocks, border strips, and binding with a rotary cutter and ruler. All measurements include ¼-inch seam allowances. To speed the cutting process, the fabrics may be layered before cutting them into strips. The strips may then be cut into the necessary number of segments.

From one of the blue or teal prints, cut:
- One 18-inch square for continuous strip bias binding. The balance of this fabric may be cut into strips for the blocks and borders.

From the light pink, blue, and teal prints, cut:
- Three hundred eighteen 1 × 1½-inch B strips
- Two hundred ten 1 × 2½-inch E strips

- Two hundred ten 1 × 3-inch F strips
- One hundred eight 1 × 4-inch I strips
- Two hundred ten 1 × 4½-inch J strips
- One hundred eight 1½ × 2-inch M strips
- One hundred eight 1½ × 2½-inch D strips
- One hundred eight 1½ × 3½-inch O strips
- One hundred eight 1½ × 4-inch H strips
- One hundred eight 1½ × 5-inch Q strips

From the medium and dark blue and teal prints, cut:
- One hundred eighty-six 1 × 1-inch A squares
- Sixty-four 1 × 2-inch N strips
- Sixty-four 1 × 2½-inch E strips
- Sixty-four 1 × 3½-inch P strips
- One hundred twenty-six 1 × 4-inch I strips
- Sixty-four 1 × 5-inch R strips
- Sixty-four 1 × 5½-inch S strips
- One hundred twenty-six 1½ × 1½-inch C squares
- One hundred twenty-six 1½ × 2½-inch D strips
- One hundred twenty-six 1½ × 3-inch G strips
- One hundred twenty-six 1½ × 4-inch H strips
- One hundred twenty-six 1½ × 4½-inch K strips
- One hundred twenty-six 1½ × 5½-inch L strips

From the fuchsia and purple prints, cut:
- One hundred twenty-eight 1 × 1-inch A squares
- Eighty-four 1 × 2½-inch E strips
- Forty-four 1 × 2-inch N strips
- Forty-four 1 × 3½-inch P strips
- Eighty-four 1 × 4-inch I strips
- Forty-four 1 × 5-inch R strips
- Eighty-four 1½ × 1½-inch C squares
- Eighty-four 1½ × 2½-inch D strips
- Eighty-four 1½ × 3-inch G strips
- Eighty-four 1½ × 4-inch H strips
- Eighty-four 1½ × 4½-inch K strips
- Eighty-four 1½ × 5½-inch L strips

From the remaining medium and dark blue, teal, fuchsia, and purple prints, cut:
- 1½-inch wide strips in varying lengths, to *total* approximately 1,700 inches, for piecing the borders

- Eight 1½-inch C squares
- Eight 1½ × 2½-inch D strips
- Eight 1½ × 3½-inch O strips
- Eight 1½ × 4½-inch K strips
- Four 1½ × 5½-inch strips L strips

Piecing the Blocks

This quilt contains 318 Log Cabin blocks in four different color variations. The illusion of curves is created by using strips in two different widths within the same block.

Sew the blocks together in the same way you would assemble any Log Cabin–style block, referring to the block diagrams as you work on each of the variations. Press all seam allowances toward the last strip added.

Piecing Block 1

Block 1 is made up of medium and dark blue and teal prints combined with light pink, blue, and teal prints.

1. Sew a dark A square to a light A square, as shown in **Diagram 1.** The dark A square will be the center of the block. Sew a light B strip to this A/A unit, trimming the B strip to match the length of the A unit, if necessary.

Diagram 1

2. Sew a dark C square to the A/A/B unit, as shown in **Diagram 2.**

Diagram 2

3. Referring to the **Block 1 Diagram,** continue adding strips, working clockwise, in the following order: a dark D strip, a light E strip, a light F strip, a dark G strip, a dark H strip, a light I strip, a light J strip, a dark K strip, and a dark L strip.

4. Make 126 of Block 1.

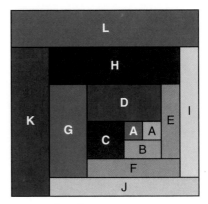

Block 1 Diagram

Piecing Block 2

Block 2 is also made up of medium and dark blue and teal prints combined with light pink, blue, and teal prints.

1. Sew a dark A square to a light B strip, as shown in **Diagram 3.** The dark A square will be the center of Block 2. Add a light M strip, followed by a dark N strip, as shown.

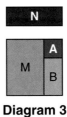

Diagram 3

2. Referring to the **Block 2 Diagram,** continue constructing Block 2 in the same manner as for Block 1, working clockwise as you add the remaining strips in the following order: a dark E strip, a light D strip, a light O strip, a dark P strip, a dark I strip, a light H strip, a light Q strip, a dark R strip, and a dark S strip. Make 64 of Block 2.

Piecing Block 3

Block 3 is made up of medium and dark fuchsia and purple prints combined with light pink, blue, and teal prints. Referring to the **Block 3 Diagram,** follow the same piecing process as for Block 1, substituting a medium or dark fuchsia or purple for the medium/dark blue/teal. Make 84 of Block 3.

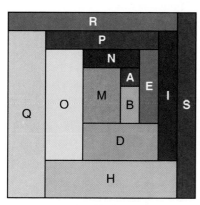

Block 2 Diagram

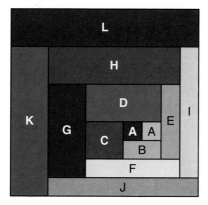

Block 3 Diagram

Piecing Block 4

Block 4 is also made up of medium and dark fuchsia and purple prints combined with light pink, blue, and teal prints. Referring to the **Block 4 Diagram,** follow the same piecing process as for Block 2, substituting a medium or dark fuchsia or purple for the medium/dark blue/teal. Make 44 of Block 4.

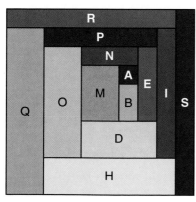

Block 4 Diagram

Assembling the Quilt Top

1. Referring to the **Quilt Diagram** on page 72 for block and color placement, lay out the Log Cabin blocks in 17 horizontal rows of 18 blocks each.

2. Sew the blocks together into 17 horizontal rows. Press the seam allowances in opposite directions between alternate rows.

3. Sew the rows of blocks together, pinning carefully to match seams. Press the seam allowances toward the top edge of the quilt top.

Piecing the Borders

1. Referring to **Diagram 4,** sew enough 1½-inch-wide strips together end to end, to create twenty 85½-inch randomly pieced lengths.

Diagram 4

2. Sew these randomly pieced lengths together to make four 5½ × 85½-inch lengths, as shown in **Diagram 5.** Two of these lengths will be used for the side borders.

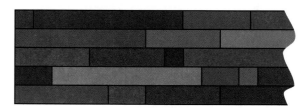

Diagram 5

3. Referring to **Diagram 5** and the **Quilt Diagram** on page 72, cut two 5½ × 40½-inch Y border units. Press the seam allowances to one side.

4. Referring to **Diagram 5** and the **Quilt Diagram,** cut two 5½ × 20½-inch Z border units. Press the seam allowances to one side.

5. Referring to the **Quilt Diagram** for block placement, complete the top border by sewing together a Z border unit, a Block 1, a Block 2, a Block 2, a Block 1, a Y border unit, a Block 1, and a Block 2, as shown. Press the seam allowances in the opposite direction from those in the top row of the quilt top.

Quilt Diagram

6. Referring to the **Quilt Diagram** for block placement, complete the bottom border in the same manner, by sewing together a Block 4, a Block 3, a Y border unit, a Block 1, a Block 2, a Block 4, a Block 3, and a Z border unit. Press the seam allowances in the opposite direction from those in the bottom row of the quilt top.

Piecing the Corner Blocks

The corner blocks are made up of 1½-inch-wide strips. These strips may be medium or dark blue, teal, purple, or fuchsia. There are no

light fabrics in the corner blocks. As you select your fabrics for these blocks, take care to include some of the same ones that appear at the ends of each of the four border strips. By using some of the same fabrics in the corner blocks, the entire border will appear to be more unified and continuous.

1. Referring to the **Corner Block Diagram,** sew two C squares together, pressing the seam allowance toward the last piece added. Sew a D strip to the right side of the two C squares, followed by another D strip at the bottom edge of the C unit, as shown.

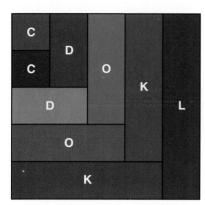

Corner Block Diagram

2. Referring to the **Corner Block Diagram,** continue constructing the block by adding an O strip to both the right and bottom edges.

3. Referring to the **Corner Block Diagram,** sew a K strip to both the right and bottom edges, as shown.

4. Sew an L strip to the right edge of the unit, completing the corner block.

5. Make four corner blocks.

Attaching the Borders to the Quilt Top

1. Referring to the **Quilt Diagram,** sew the top and bottom borders to the quilt top, taking care to align block seams where necessary. Press the seam allowances toward the edge of the quilt.

2. Referring to the **Quilt Diagram** for placement, sew a corner square at each end of the left and right border strips. Press the seam allowances away from the corner squares.

3. Sew left and right side borders to the proper side edges of the quilt top, making certain that they are positioned correctly. Press the seam allowances toward the outer edge of the quilt.

Quilting and Finishing

1. Mark quilting designs as desired. The quilt shown is quilted in an overall pattern that generally follows the curves in the pieced design. The **Quilting Diagram** indicates the quilting design.

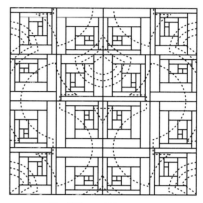

Quilting Diagram

2. Divide the backing fabric into three equal 108-inch-long pieces. Remove the selvages and sew the pieces together along the long edges, creating a three-panel quilt back. Press these seams open and place them so that they will lie parallel to the top and bottom of the quilt.

3. Layer the quilt back, batting, and quilt top. The backing fabric should extend equally beyond all edges of the quilt top, so that the quilt back is centered. Baste; then trim the quilt back to approximately 3 inches larger than the quilt top on all sides. Quilt all marked designs and add any additional quilting as desired.

4. From each of the binding fabrics, make approximately 200 inches of double-fold, continuous bias binding. Sew these two long strips together with a diagonal seam. For more information on making and attaching continuous bias binding, see page 164.

5. Sew the binding to the quilt top. Trim the excess backing and batting. Using matching thread and an invisible stitch, hand finish the binding on the back of the quilt.

Hexagons

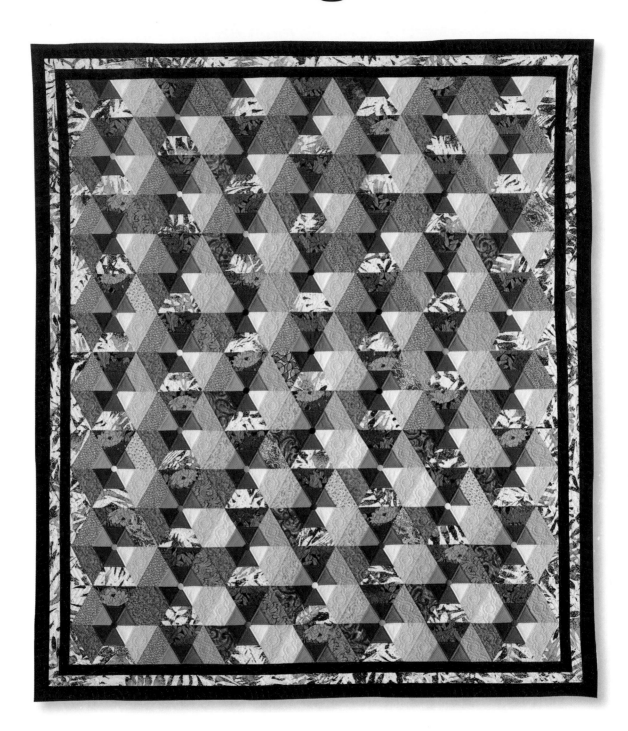

Quiltmaker: Betty Patty

Inspired by a photo in *Quilter's Newsletter Magazine,* Betty reached into her scrap bag and tapped her vivid imagination to come up with this delightful takeoff on a time-honored hexagonal design. The center circles are appliquéd, which makes them appear to be slightly stuffed.

Skill Level: Easy

Size: Finished quilt is 76 × 88¾ inches
Equilateral triangle unit is 6 inches finished

Fabrics and Supplies

✓ 2½ yards of black solid fabric for the inner and outer borders and binding

✓ 2½ yards of large-scale black and white print fabric for the triangle units and middle borders

✓ ¾ yard of large-scale, multicolored floral print fabric for the triangle units

✓ Fabric scraps *totaling* ¾ yard in teal or green leafy prints for the triangle units

✓ Fabric scraps *totaling* ¾ yard in yellow small-scale floral prints for the triangle units

✓ Fabric scraps *totaling* ¾ yard in dusty pink floral prints for the triangle units

✓ Fabric scraps *totaling* ¾ yard in light blue spotty prints for the triangle units

✓ ⅔ yard *each* of dark green solid, bright red solid, light yellow solid, medium pink solid, deep fucshia solid, and medium blue solid fabrics for the triangle units

✓ 2⅔ yards of 90-inch-wide unbleached muslin (or 5¼ yards of 45-inch wide fabric) for the quilt back

✓ Queen-size batting (90 × 108 inches)

✓ Rotary cutter, ruler, and mat

✓ Template material

Cutting

Instructions are for quick cutting the borders and binding with a rotary cutter and ruler. These measurements include ¼-inch seam allowances. Measurements for the borders are longer than needed; trim them to the exact length when adding them to the quilt top.

Full-size patterns for pieces A through D are given on page 79. Except for the D appliqué pattern piece, ¼-inch seam allowances are included. Add the seam allowance to pattern piece D when cutting it out of the fabric. Transfer pattern pieces to template material. To cut out the C reverse pieces from fabric, simply flip the C template over, so that the wrong side is facing up as you trace around it. Refer to page 153 for tips on making and using templates.

From the black solid, cut:
• Two 2 × 78-inch inner border strips
• Two 2 × 90-inch inner border strips
• Two 2½ × 78-inch outer border strips
• Two 2½ × 90-inch outer border strips
• Four 2½ × 90-inch strips for straight-grain binding

From the large-scale, black and white print, cut:
• Two 2 × 78-inch middle border strips
• Two 2 × 90-inch middle border strips
• 53 B pieces
• 15 C triangles
• 15 C reverse triangles

From the large-scale, multicolored floral print, cut:
• 52 B pieces

From the teal and green print scraps, cut:
• 53 B pieces

From the yellow print scraps, cut:
• 53 B pieces

From the pink print scraps, cut:
• 52 B pieces

From the blue print scraps, cut:
• 52 B pieces

From each of the green, red, and yellow solids, cut:
• 53 A triangles

From each of the pink, fuchsia, and blue solids, cut:
• 52 A triangles

From the remaining scraps of solid fabrics (including the black solid), cut:
• 49 D circles

Piecing the Triangle Units

This quilt requires a total of 315 triangle units. Each triangle unit is made up of one A triangle and one B piece. There are six different color combinations for the triangle units in the quilt shown, as indicated in the **Block Key Diagram.** For each triangle unit, press the seam allowances toward the B piece.

Assembling the Rows

This quilt consists of 15 horizontal rows of triangle units. Each row has 21 triangle units in different color combinations.

1. For Row 1, use the six color combinations of triangle units, as shown in **Diagram 1** and the quilt photograph on page 74. Lay out the 21 triangle units, placing a black and white C triangle at one end and a black and white C reverse triangle at the opposite end.

2. Sew the 21 triangle units, C, and C reverse triangles together to complete Row 1. Press all of the seam allowances toward the left. Make a total of eight Row 1s.

3. For Row 2, refer to the triangle units shown in **Diagram 2** and the quilt photograph. Lay out the 21 triangle units, placing a black and

white C triangle at one end of the row and a black and white C reverse triangle at the opposite end of the row.

4. Sew the 21 triangle units, C, and C reverse triangles together to complete Row 2. Press all of the seam allowances toward the right. Make a total of seven Row 2s.

Assembling the Quilt Top

1. Lay out the 15 horizontal rows of the quilt, alternating Rows 1 and 2, as shown in the **Quilt Diagram.**

2. Sew the rows together, pinning carefully to match the seams. Press all of the seam allowances toward the top edge of the quilt.

3. Prepare the D circles according to your preferred method of hand appliqué. For more information on appliqué, see page 157. Appliqué a D circle at every juncture of six A triangles, as shown in the **Quilt Diagram.** The seam allowances underneath the D circles will give the appliqués a slightly three-dimensional look.

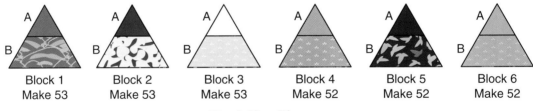

Block 1
Make 53

Block 2
Make 53

Block 3
Make 53

Block 4
Make 52

Block 5
Make 52

Block 6
Make 52

Block Key Diagram

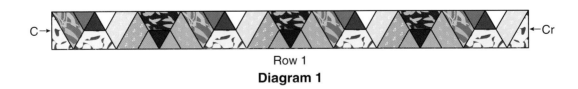

Row 1
Diagram 1

Row 2
Diagram 2

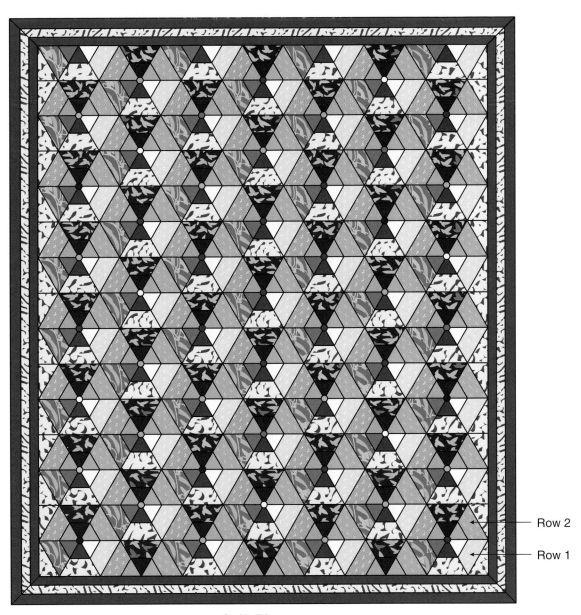

Row 2

Row 1

Quilt Diagram

Attaching the Borders

1. To make the border units for the top and bottom edges of the quilt, sew together a 2 × 78-inch black solid inner border strip, a 2 × 78-inch black and white print middle border strip, and a 2½ × 78-inch black solid border outer strip, referring to the **Quilt Diagram** for the correct placement. Press all of the seam allowances toward the black solid borders. Make two of these border units.

2. Referring to the **Quilt Diagram,** make the border units for the side edges of the quilt in the same manner, sewing together the 90-inch-long black solid and black and white print strips.

3. Referring to the **Quilt Diagram,** sew the four border units to the appropriate edges of the quilt top, beginning and ending each seam ¼ inch from the edge of the quilt top. Miter the corner seams, trimming excess fabric from each corner seam and pressing these seams open. For more information on mitering, see page 160.

Quilting and Finishing

1. Mark quilting designs as desired. The quilt shown has outline quilting around each of the A triangles and in the ditch around each D circle as well as around each of the large hexagons. In the C and C reverse triangles, parallel lines are quilted at ½-inch intervals. The borders are quilted as shown in the **Border Quilting Diagram.** The full-size pattern for the cable quilting design in pattern piece B is on given below.

2. If you choose to use 45-inch-wide fabric for the quilt back, cut it into two equal lengths. Trim the selvage edges and sew the two pieces together along the long edges. Press this seam open.

3. Layer the quilt back, batting, and quilt top; baste. Trim the quilt back and batting to approximately 3 inches larger than the quilt top on all sides.

4. Quilt all marked designs.

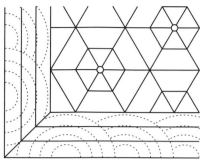

Border Quilting Diagram

5. From the 2½ × 90-inch strips of black solid fabric, make approximately 340 inches of double-fold, straight-grain binding. For instructions on making and attaching binding, see page 164.

6. Sew the binding to the quilt top. Trim the excess batting and backing. Using a thread color that matches the binding fabric, use a blind stitch to hand finish the binding on the back of the quilt.

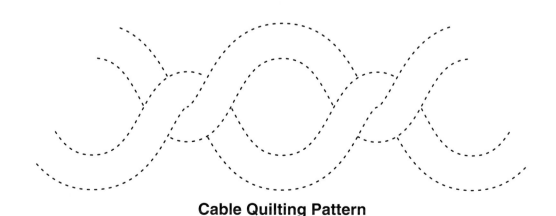

Cable Quilting Pattern

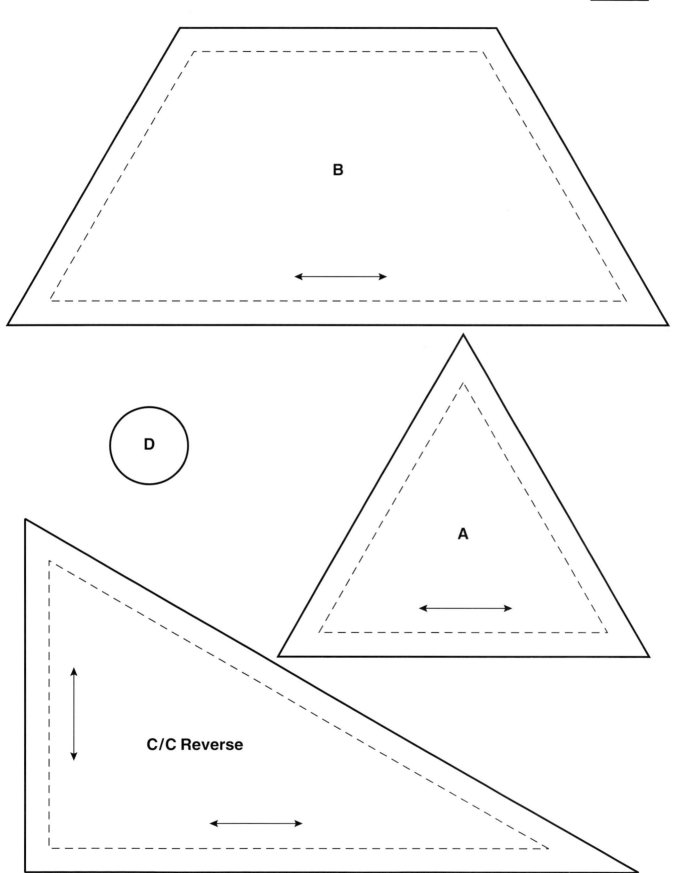

B

D

A

C/C Reverse

Konnichiwa

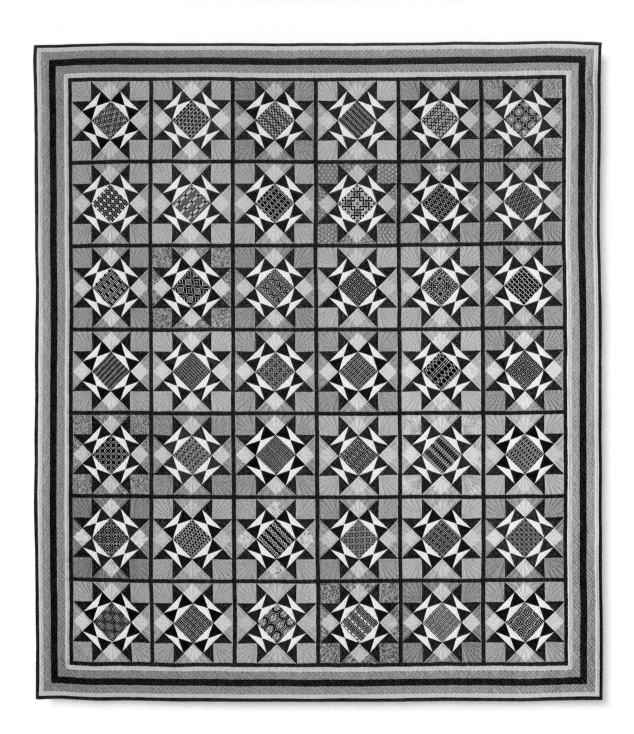

Quiltmaker: Suzanne Marshall

Konnichiwa is a Japanese greeting meaning "Good afternoon." Suzanne's collection of blue and white oriental batik-style prints form the basis for this clean, graphic quilt design. The use of cool gray as the background neutral provides an unexpected—and elegant—touch.

Skill Level: Intermediate

Size: Finished quilt is 85½ × 98 inches
Finished block is 12 inches square

Fabrics and Supplies

NOTE: The yardages listed are for cutting each of the border and vertical sashing strips in the quilt as a single length of fabric.

✓ 2⅞ yards of dark red print fabric for the sashing strips, borders, and binding

✓ 2⅞ yards of light gray print fabric for the blocks and borders

✓ 2⅞ yards of medium gray print fabric for the blocks and borders

✓ 2 yards of white-on-white print fabric for the blocks

✓ 1¼ yards of navy blue print fabric for the blocks

✓ Scraps of 42 assorted dark red print fabrics for the blocks. An 8 × 8-inch piece of each is sufficient.

✓ Scraps of 20 assorted medium gray print fabrics for the blocks. A 14 × 18-inch piece of each is sufficient.

✓ Scraps of six assorted light gray print fabrics for the blocks. A 14 × 18-inch piece of each is sufficient.

✓ Scraps of assorted indigo and white or navy and white batik print fabrics. There are 42 blocks in this quilt. Each block requires a 4¾-inch cut center square. You may use all different fabrics or duplicate as desired.

✓ 7½ yards of fabric for the quilt back

✓ Queen-size quilt batting (90 × 108 inches)

✓ Rotary cutter, ruler, and mat

✓ Template material

Cutting

All measurements include ¼-inch seam allowances. Measurements for the borders are longer than needed; trim them to the necessary length when they are added to the quilt top. With the exception of pattern pieces A and B, instructions given are for quick cutting using a rotary cutter and ruler. In most cases, strips for rotary cutting are cut slightly longer than needed to allow for adjustment or error in cutting.

Make templates for A and B using the full-size pattern pieces on page 85. Cut pieces in the order listed.

From the 2⅞ yards of dark red print fabric, cut:
- Two 1½ × 102-inch strips for borders
- Two 1½ × 90-inch strips for borders
- Four 2½-inch strips lengthwise for the binding
- Five 1 × 90-inch strips for sashings
- Two 1 × 90-inch strips for borders
- Two 1 × 102-inch strips for borders
- Five 1 × 102-inch strips for sashing. Cut these strips into 1 × 12½-inch segments. You'll need a total of 36 segments.

From the 2⅞ yards of light gray print fabric, cut:
- Two 1¼ × 102-inch border strips
- Two 1¼ × 90-inch border strips
- One 2⅝ × 66-inch strip. Cut this strip into 2⅝-inch squares to make a total of 24 D squares.

From the 2⅞ yards of medium gray print fabric, cut:
- Two 1¾ × 102-inch border strips
- Two 1¾ × 90-inch border strips
- One 3½ × 30-inch strip. Cut this strip into eight 3½-inch squares to make a total of 8 F squares.
- One 4¼ × 18-inch strip. Cut this strip into four 4¼-inch squares; cut these squares in half diagonally in both directions to make 16 E triangles.

From the 2 yards of white-on-white print fabric, cut:
- 336 B triangles, using template B

From the 1¼ yards of navy blue print fabric, cut:
- Ten 4¼ × 44-inch strips. Cut these strips into eighty-four 4¼-inch squares; cut these squares in half diagonally in both directions to make 336 E triangles.

From the assorted dark red print scraps, cut:

• 336 A triangles in groups of 8, using template A

From each of the assorted medium gray scraps, cut:

• Two 3½ × 18-inch strips. Cut these strips into 3½-inch F squares. You'll need a total of 8 F squares from *each* fabric.

• One 4¼ × 18-inch strip. Cut this strip into four 4¼-inch squares; cut these squares in half diagonally in both directions to make 16 E triangles from *each* fabric.

From each of the assorted light gray print scraps, cut:

• Five 2⅝ × 14-inch strips. Cut these strips into 2⅝-inch D squares. You'll need a total of 24 D squares from *each* fabric.

From the assorted indigo and white or navy and white print scraps, cut:

• Forty-two 4¾-inch C squares.

Piecing the Blocks

1. Referring to the **Block Diagram,** lay out the following pieces for one block: eight matching red A triangles, eight white B triangles, one indigo and white C square, four matching light gray D squares, eight navy E triangles, four matching medium gray E triangles, and four matching medium gray F squares.

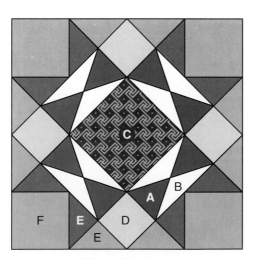

Block Diagram

2. Sew a red A triangle to a white B triangle, as shown in **Diagram 1.** Make eight of these units. Press the seam allowances toward the A pieces.

Diagram 1

3. Sew together two A/B units, as shown in **Diagram 2.** Make four of these units, pressing the seam allowance to one side.

Diagram 2

4. Sew a D square to each side of one of the A/B units, as shown in **Diagram 3.** Make two of these rows and press the seam allowances away from the D squares.

Diagram 3

5. Sew the remaining A/B units to each side of a C square as shown in **Diagram 4.** Press the seam allowance away from the C square, grading the seam allowance if necessary. For instructions on grading seam allowances, see page 155.

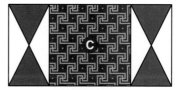

Diagram 4

6. Sew the rows together, as shown in **Diagram 5,** pinning carefully to match the seams. Press the seam allowances toward the center of the block.

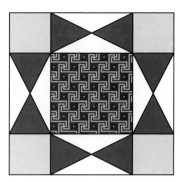

Diagram 5

7. Sew a navy E triangle to either side of an F square as shown in **Diagram 6.** Make four of these E/F units, pressing the seam allowances away from the F square.

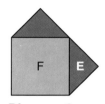

Diagram 6

8. Attach a gray E triangle to either side of each of the E/F units, as shown in **Diagram 7.** Press the seam allowances toward the gray E triangles.

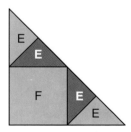

Diagram 7

9. Referring to the **Block Diagram,** sew one of the E/F triangle units to each side of the center block, pinning carefully to match the seams. Press the seam allowances toward the E/F triangle units. Make a total of 42 blocks.

Assembling the Quilt Top

1. Referring to the **Quilt Diagram** on page 84, lay out the blocks in six vertical rows of seven blocks each. Insert a 1 × 12½-inch sashing strip between each block in each row. Sew the blocks and sashes together to complete the rows, trimming the seam allowances as necessary and pressing them away from the blocks.

2. Measure each of the completed vertical rows and take an average measurement. Trim the 1 × 89-inch sashing strips to this average measurement. Referring to the **Quilt Diagram,** insert a trimmed sashing strip between each of the vertical rows. Sew the rows and sashing strips together, taking care to align blocks horizontally before pinning and stitching. Ease as necessary for a proper fit. Trim the seam allowances as needed and press them away from the blocks.

Assembling and Adding the Borders

1. Referring to the **Border Diagram,** sew together along the long edge of the fabric, in order: a 1 × 90-inch dark red border strip, a 1¼ × 90-inch light gray border strip, a 1¾ × 90-inch medium gray border strip, a 1½ × 90-inch dark red border strip, a 1¾ × 90-inch medium gray border strip, and a 1¼ × 90-inch light gray border strip. Press all the seam allowances toward the dark red center strip. Make two of these border units, label them "top and bottom" and set them aside.

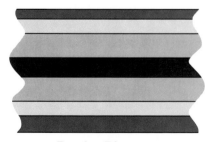

Border Diagram

2. Make two border units with the remaining 102-inch-long red and gray border strips, sewing them together in the order listed in Step 1. Label these units "left and right" and set them aside.

3. Sew the borders to the appropriate sides of the quilt, mitering each corner. For instructions on mitering, see page 160.

Quilt Diagram

Quilting and Finishing

1. Each block in this quilt is quilted in a simple pattern of carefully placed straight lines, and the borders are quilted in a combination of straight lines and a cable design, as shown in the **Border Quilting Diagram** and the **Block Quilting Diagram.**

Border Quilting Diagram

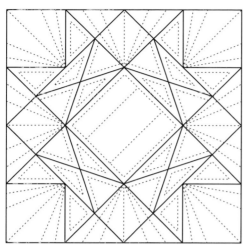

Block Quilting Diagram

2. Divide the backing fabric into three equal 90-inch-long pieces. Remove the selvages and sew the pieces together along the long edges. The seams will run parallel to the top and bottom of the quilt. Press the seams open.

3. Layer the quilt back, batting and quilt top. The backing fabric should extend beyond the quilt top equally, so that the center panel is centered. Baste the layers together and trim the quilt back and batting so that they are approximately 3 inches larger than the quilt top on all sides.

4. Quilt all marked designs and add additional quilting as desired. The quilt shown is quilted in navy blue quilting thread.

5. From the binding fabric, make approximately 380 inches of double-fold, straight-grain binding. The binding on the quilt shown finishes ½ inch wide, balancing the narrow red sashing and borders strips that are cut from the same fabric. To achieve this effect, cut binding strips 2½ inches wide. See page 164 for details on making and attaching binding.

6. Sew the binding to the quilt top. Trim the excess backing and batting, and use matching thread and an invisible stitch to hand finish the binding on the back of the quilt.

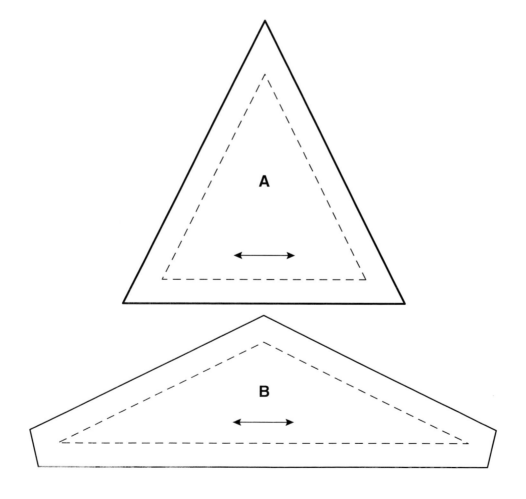

HOMESPUN PLAIDS

Stargazing with Roberta

Quiltmaker: Karen Hull Sienk

Contemporary plaids from the Roberta Horton collection create a country star quilt made from just two blocks—the Sawtooth Star and Shoo-Fly. Karen's careful attention to placing different color values next to each other have filled this beautiful quilt with sparkle and light. Choose either the bed-size or miniature version to complement your decor.

Skill Level: Easy

Size: Finished quilt is 64½ × 88½ inches
Finished blocks are 8 inches square
(Directions for miniature quilt begin on
page 94.)

Fabrics and Supplies

This quilt contains approximately eight different light background plaids and 18 different medium or dark plaids. The yardages are generous enough to allow for flexibility in cutting and color placement. If you use more or fewer fabrics in your quilt, you may wish to adjust the yardages accordingly. Just for fun, try including some plaids from used men's shirts—or add a few flannel plaids to create intriguing visual texture.

✓ 1½ yards of black striped fabric for the outer border

✓ 1 yard of assorted white striped and light plaid fabrics for the first and fourth borders

✓ ½ yard of blue striped fabric for the second border

✓ Assorted dark and medium plaid and striped fabrics *totaling* approximately 3 yards for the blocks and Sawtooth borders

✓ Assorted light plaid and striped fabrics *totaling* 2½ yards for the backgrounds in the blocks

✓ Full-size batting (81 × 96 inches)

✓ 5½ yards of fabric for the quilt back

✓ Assorted scraps of dark and medium plaid and striped fabrics for the binding

✓ Rotary cutter, ruler, and mat

Cutting

This quilt requires 27 Sawtooth Star blocks and 27 Shoo-Fly blocks, a pieced Sawtooth border, as well as two pieced scrap borders.

Instructions are for quick cutting the pieces with a rotary cutter and ruler. Note that quick cutting may result in leftover pieces. These measurements include ¼-inch seam allowances. Except for the Sawtooth border, the other borders will be longer than needed; trim them to the correct length when adding them to the quilt top.

For the Sawtooth Star Blocks
From the light plaid and striped fabrics, cut:
- Seven 2½ × 45-inch strips. Cut these strips into one hundred eight 2½-inch C squares, in matching sets of 4.
- Four 5¼ × 45-inch strips. Cut these strips into twenty-seven 5¼-inch squares; cut these squares in half diagonally in both directions to make 108 A triangles, in matching sets of 4.

From the medium or dark plaid and striped fabrics, cut:
- Three 4½ × 45-inch strips. Cut these strips into twenty-seven 4½-inch D squares.
- Eight 2⅞ × 45-inch strips. Cut these strips into one hundred eight 2⅞-inch squares. Cut these squares in half diagonally to make 216 B triangles, in matching sets of 8.

For the Shoo-Fly Blocks
From the light plaid and striped fabrics, cut:
- Four 2⅞ × 45-inch strips. Cut these strips into fifty-four 2⅞-inch squares; cut these squares in half diagonally in both directions to make 108 B triangles, in matching sets of 4.

From the medium and dark plaid and striped fabrics, cut:
- Three 4½ × 45-inch strips. Cut these strips into twenty-seven 4½-inch D squares.
- Four 2⅞ × 45-inch strips. Cut these strips into fifty-four 2⅞-inch squares; cut these squares in half diagonally in both directions to make 108 B triangles, in matching sets of 4.
- Thirteen 2½ × 44-inch strips. Cut these strips into 2½ × 4½-inch rectangles. You will need a total of 108 E rectangles in matching sets of 4.

For the Sawtooth Borders
From the light plaid and striped fabrics, cut:
- Two 5¼ × 45-inch strips. Cut these strips into sixteen 5¼-inch squares; cut these squares in half diagonally in both directions to make 64 A triangles.
- Two 2⅞-inch light squares. Cut these squares in half diagonally to make four B triangles.

From the medium and dark plaid and striped fabrics, cut:
- Five 2⅞ × 45-inch strips. Cut these strips into sixty-six 2⅞-inch squares; cut these squares in half diagonally to make 132 B triangles.

From the black striped fabric, cut:
- Two 3½ × 60-inch border strips
- Two 3½ × 90-inch border strips

From the blue striped fabric, cut:
- Two 1½ × 52-inch border strips
- Two 1½ × 78-inch border strips

From the assorted white or light striped and plaid fabrics, cut:
- Thirty 1½ × 9½-inch strips for the first border
- Thirty-four 1½ × 9½-inch strips for the fourth border

From the backing fabric, cut:
- Two 35 × 94-inch pieces

From the assorted scraps of dark and medium plaid and striped fabrics, cut:
- Enough pieces that are 2½ inches wide and various lengths to total approximately 340 inches for the pieced binding.

Piecing the Sawtooth Star Blocks

1. Referring to **Diagram 1,** sew a dark B triangle to each side of an A triangle. Press the seam allowances away from the A triangles. Make a total of 108 of these units, remembering that each Sawtooth Star block requires a set of four of these units that match each other.

Diagram 1

2. Referring to **Diagram 2,** sew a C square to each end of one unit, as shown. Each Sawtooth Star block requires four matching C squares. Make a total of 54 of these rows. Reserve the remanining 54 units for the sides of the Sawtooth Star block.

Diagram 2

3. Referring to the **Sawtooth Star Block Diagram,** sew two of the units from Step 1 to each side of a D center square, as shown. Sew two of the rows with C corner squares to the top and bottom edges, completing the Sawtooth Star block, as shown.

4. Make 27 Sawtooth Star blocks.

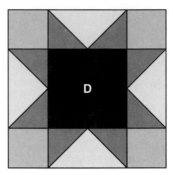

Sawtooth Star Block Diagram

Piecing the Shoo-Fly Blocks

1. Referring to **Diagram 3,** sew a light B triangle to a dark B triangle, as shown. Press the seam allowances toward the darker fabric. Each Shoo-Fly block requires four sets of these light/dark triangle-pieced squares in matching fabrics.

2. Referring to **Diagram 4,** sew two matching triangle-pieced B squares to an E rectangle, as shown. Press the seam allowances toward the E rectangle. Each Shoo-Fly block requires two of these rows in matching fabrics.

Diagram 3   **Diagram 4**

3. Referring to **Diagram 5,** sew an E rectangle that matches the rectangle used in Step 2 to each side of a D center square, as shown. Press the seam allowances toward the E rectangles.

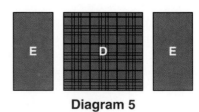

Diagram 5

4. Referring to the **Shoo-Fly Block Diagram,** sew the three rows together, completing the Shoo-Fly block. Make 27 Shoo-Fly blocks.

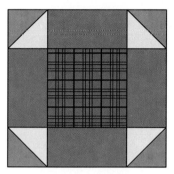

Shoo-Fly Block Diagram

Assembling the Quilt Top

1. Referring to the **Quilt Diagram** on page 92 for block placement, sew the Sawtooth Star and Shoo-Fly blocks together into nine horizontal rows of six blocks each. Press the seam allowances in opposite directions between blocks.

2. Referring to the **Quilt Diagram,** sew the nine horizontal rows of blocks together. Press the seam allowances in alternate directions between rows.

Making and Attaching the Borders

Piecing the First Border

1. Sew together six light 1½ × 9½-inch rectangles to form the top and bottom inner scrap borders. Press the seam allowances to one side.

2. Sew together nine 1½ × 9½-inch rectangles to form the side inner scrap borders. Press the seam allowances to one side.

3. Referring to the **Quilt Diagram** on page 92, sew the top and bottom inner scrap borders to the quilt top, trimming the ends of the borders even with the edge of the quilt top. Press the seam allowances toward the borders.

4. In the same manner, sew the side inner scrap borders to the quilt top and trim them even with the edges of the quilt top. Press the seam allowances toward the borders.

Attaching the Second Border

1. Sew the two 1½ × 52-inch blue striped border strips to the top and bottom edges of the quilt top, trimming them even with the edges of the quilt top. Press the seam allowances toward these borders.

2. Sew the two 1½ × 78-inch blue striped border strips to the sides of the quilt top, trimming them in the same manner. Press the seam allowances toward these borders.

Piecing the Sawtooth Borders

1. Referring to **Diagram 1,** sew a dark or medium B triangle to each side of an A triangle, as shown. The Sawtooth border requires a total of 64 of these light/dark triangle-pieced units.

2. Referring to the **Sawtooth Border Diagram,** sew together a row of 13 triangle-pieced units for each of the top and bottom Sawtooth borders. Press the seam allowances to one side.

3. Sew these top and bottom Sawtooth borders to the top and bottom edges of the quilt top. Press the seam allowances toward the blue striped borders.

4. Referring to the **Sawtooth Border Diagram,** sew together a row of 19 triangle-pieced units for each side Sawtooth border. Press the seam allowances to one side.

Top and Bottom Borders

Side Borders

Sawtooth Border Diagram

Quilt Diagram

5. Referring to **Diagram 3** on page 90, sew a light B triangle to a dark B triangle, as shown. Repeat to make three more of these triangle-pieced B squares. Sew a light/dark B triangle-pieced square to each end of the side Sawtooth borders. Press the seam allowances to one side.

6. Sew these side Sawtooth borders to the sides of the quilt top. Press the seam allowances toward the second borders.

Piecing the Fourth Border

1. Referring to the **Quilt Diagram**, sew seven light plaid or striped 1½ × 9½-inch rectan-

gles together for the pieced scrap outer borders that will be sewn to the top and bottom edges of the quilt top. Press the seam allowances to one side.

2. Referring to the **Quilt Diagram,** sew together ten light plaid or striped 1½ × 9½-inch rectangles for the pieced scrap outer borders that will be sewn to the sides of the quilt top. Press the seam allowances to one side.

3. Sew the top and bottom pieced scrap outer borders to the quilt top, trimming the ends of the borders even with the edge of the quilt top. Press the seam allowances toward these borders.

4. Sew the side pieced scrap outer borders to the quilt top, trimming the ends of the borders in the same manner. Press the seam allowances toward these borders.

Attaching the Outer Borders

1. Sew the two 3½ × 60-inch black striped border strips to the top and bottom edges of the quilt top and trim them even with the edge of the quilt top. Press the seam allowances toward the black striped borders.

2. Sew the two 3½ × 90-inch black striped border strips to the side edges of the quilt top, trimming them in the same manner. Press the seam allowances toward the black striped borders.

Quilting and Finishing

1. Mark quilting designs as desired. The Sawtooth and Shoo-Fly blocks in the quilt shown are quilted as indicated in the **Quilting Diagram.** The first and second borders are quilted ¼ inch away from the outer edges. The Sawtooth border is quilted ¼ inch away from the pieced triangle units. The fourth and outer borders are quilted in straight lines at 2-inch intervals and have diagonal lines of quilting at the corners that give these borders the visual illusion of mitered seams.

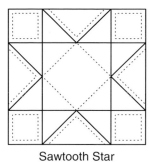 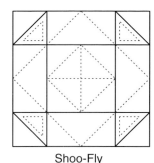

Sawtooth Star   Shoo-Fly

Quilting Diagram

2. Trim the selvages from the two pieces of backing fabric and sew them together along the long edge. Press this seam open.

3. Layer the quilt back, batting, and quilt top; baste. Trim the quilt back and batting 3 inches larger than the quilt top on all sides.

4. Quilt all marked quilting designs and add any additional quilting designs desired.

5. Place the binding strips together, end to end, alternating shorter strips with longer strips. Sew the strips together with diagonal seams to create approximately 320 inches of decorative binding. Press the seams open and trim them to ¼ inch, if necessary, to reduce bulk in the binding.

6. Attach the binding to the quilt top; turn it to the back and hand finish with an invisible stitch. For more information on making and attaching binding, see page 164.

Stargazing with Roberta Miniature

Size: Finished quilt is 32 × 40 inches Finished blocks are 4 inches square (shown in the photograph on page 88)

Fabrics and Supplies

This quilt requires approximately eight different light or medium plaid or striped fabrics and 18 different medium or dark plaid or striped fabrics. Instructions are for quick cutting the pieces with a rotary cutter and ruler. These measurements include ¼-inch seam allowances. The yardages are generous enough to allow for flexibility in cutting and color placement. If you decide to use more or fewer fabrics in your quilt, you may wish to adjust the yardages accordingly.

✓ ¾ yard of black striped fabric for the outer borders

✓ ⅓ yard of white striped fabric for the first and third borders

✓ ¼ yard of red striped fabric for the second border

✓ Assorted dark and medium plaid and striped fabrics *totaling* approximately 1½ yards for the blocks and Sawtooth borders

✓ Assorted light plaid and striped fabrics *totaling* approximately 1 yard for the backgrounds in the blocks

✓ 1¼ yards of fabric for the quilt back

✓ Crib-size batting (45 × 60 inches)

✓ Rotary cutter, ruler, and mat

Cutting

This quilt requires 18 Sawtooth Star blocks, 17 Shoo-Fly blocks, and one Sawtooth border, in addition to the four other borders. Instructions are for quick cutting the pieces with a rotary cutter and ruler. Note that quick cutting may result in leftover pieces. These measurements include ¼-inch seam allowances. Except for the Sawtooth border, the borders will be longer than needed; trim them to the correct length when adding them to the quilt top.

For the Sawtooth Star Blocks

From the light plaid and striped fabrics, cut:

• Three 1½ × 45-inch strips. Cut these strips into seventy-two 1½-inch C squares, in matching sets of 4.

• Two 3¼ × 45-inch strips. Cut these strips into eighteen 3¼-inch squares; cut these squares in half diagonally in both directions to make 72 A triangles, in matching sets of 4.

From the dark plaid and striped fabrics, cut:

• Two 2½ × 45-inch strips. Cut these strips into eighteen 2½-inch D squares.

• Two 1⅞ × 45-inch strips. Cut theses strips into thirty-six 1⅞-inch squares; cut these squares in half diagonally in both directions to make 144 B triangles, in matching sets of 8.

For the Shoo-Fly Blocks

From the light or medium plaid and striped fabrics, cut:

• Seventeen 1⅞-inch squares. Cut these squares in half diagonally in both directions to make 68 B triangles, in matching sets of 4.

From the medium or dark plaid or striped fabrics, cut:

• One 1⅞ × 45-inch strip. Cut this strip into seventeen 1⅞-inch squares; cut these squares in half diagonally in both directions to make 68 B triangles, in matching sets of 4.

• Five 1½ × 45-inch strips. Cut these strips into sixty-eight 1½ × 2½-inch E rectangles, in matching sets of 4.

• Two 2½ × 45-inch strips. Cut these strips into seventeen 2½-inch D squares.

For the Sawtooth Borders

From the light or medium plaid or striped fabrics, cut:

- Two 3¼ × 45-inch strips. Cut these strips into thirteen 3¼-inch squares; cut these squares in half diagonally in both directions to make 52 A triangles.
- Two 1⅞-inch squares. Cut these squares in half diagonally for to make 4 B triangles.

From the medium or dark plaid or striped fabrics, cut:

- One 1⅞ × 45-inch strip. Cut this strip into fourteen 1⅞-inch squares; cut these squares in half diagonally to make 56 B triangles.

From the black striped fabric, cut:

- Two 3½ × 26½-inch top and bottom border strips
- Two 3½ × 40½-inch side border strips

From the white striped fabric, cut:

- Two 1½ × 24½-inch top and bottom border strips
- Two 1½ × 35½-inch side border strips
- Two 1 × 20½-inch top and bottom border strips
- Two 1 × 29½-inch side border strips

From the red striped fabric, cut:

- Two 1½ × 31½-inch top and bottom border strips
- Two 1¼ × 22½-inch side border strips

From the assorted scraps of dark and medium plaid and striped fabrics, cut:

- Enough pieces 2½ inches wide and of varying lengths to total approximately 180 inches for the binding.

Piecing the Sawtooth Star Blocks

1. Follow the same piecing sequence for the larger Sawtooth Star blocks. This is described on page 90.

2. Make a total of eighteen 4-inch Sawtooth Star blocks for this miniature version of Stargazing with Roberta.

Piecing the Shoo-Fly Blocks

1. Follow the same piecing sequence for the larger Shoo-Fly blocks. This is described on pages 90–91.

2. Make a total of seventeen 4-inch Sawtooth Star blocks for this miniature quilt.

Assembling the Quilt Top

Referring to the **Quilt Diagram** for block placement, sew the Sawtooth Star and Shoo-Fly blocks together into seven horizontal rows of five blocks each, as shown.

Quilt Diagram

Piecing the Sawtooth Borders

1. Follow the same piecing sequence for the larger basic border triangle unit, as shown on pages 91–92.

2. Referring to the **Quilt Diagram**, sew together 15 of these triangle units for each of the two side Sawtooth borders, as shown. Press the seam allowances to one side.

3. Sew together 11 of these triangle-pieced units for each of the top and bottom Sawtooth borders.

4. Referring to **Diagram 3** on page 90, sew a light B triangle to a dark B triangle, as shown. Repeat to make three more of these triangle-pieced B squares. Sew a light/dark B triangle-pieced square to each end of the side Sawtooth borders. Press the seam allowances to one side.

Attaching the Borders to the Quilt Top

The borders on this quilt are slightly different from those for the larger version. Refer to the **Quilt Diagram** on page 95 as you attach each of the borders to the quilt top and press all seam allowances toward the border strips, unless otherwise specified.

1. Sew the white striped 1 × 20½-inch top and bottom border strips to the top and bottom edges of the quilt top.

2. Sew the white striped 1 × 29½-inch side border strips to the side edges of the quilt top.

3. Sew the red striped 1½ × 31½-inch top and bottom border strips to the top and bottom edges of the quilt top.

4. Sew the red striped 1¼ × 22½-inch side border strips to the side edges of the quilt top.

5. Sew the top and bottom Sawtooth borders to the top and bottom edges of the quilt top. Press the seams toward the red borders.

6. Sew the side Sawtooth borders to the side edges of the quilt top. Press these seam allowances toward the red borders.

7. Sew the white striped 1½ × 24½-inch top and bottom border strips to the top and bottom edges of the quilt top. Press these seam allowances toward the red borders.

8. Sew the white striped 1½ × 35½-inch side border strips to the side edges of the quilt top. Press the seams toward the red borders.

9. Sew the top and bottom black striped border strips to the top and bottom edges of the quilt top.

10. Sew the side black striped border strips to the sides of the quilt top.

Quilting and Finishing

1. Mark quilting designs as desired. The Sawtooth and Shoo-Fly blocks in the quilt shown are quilted as indicated in the **Quilting Diagram.** The first white striped borders are quilted in a straight line through the center. The red striped borders are quilted ¼ inch from the inner edges. The Sawtooth borders are quilted in the ditch along each A triangle. The fourth and outer borders are quilted ¼ inch from the inner edges, and there are straight lines of quilting that extend from the seams between each of the B triangles in the Sawtooth borders to the outer edges of the quilt.

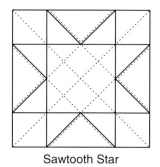 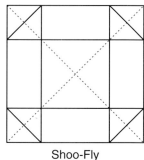

Sawtooth Star　　　　　Shoo-Fly

Quilting Diagram

2. Layer the quilt top, batting and back; baste. Trim the excess back and batting to approximately 3 inches larger than the quilt top.

3. Quilt all marked quilting designs and add any additional quilting desired.

4. Place the binding strips together, end to end, shorter strips alternating with longer strips. Sew the strips together with diagonal seams to create approximately 160 inches of decorative binding. Press these seams open and trim them to ¼ inch to reduce bulk in the binding.

5. Attach the binding to the quilt top; turn it to the back and hand finish with an invisible stitch. For more information on making and attaching binding, see page 164.

Escargot in Plaid

Quiltmaker: Shelby Morris

Shelby's sense of humor—and adventure—bubbles to the surface in this lively interpretation of the traditional Snail's Trail
pattern. A wealth of plaid fabrics lends a country flavor to this
easy-to-piece quilt. Use your rotary cutter and sewing machine
to make one for your favorite teenager.

Skill Level: Easy

Size: Finished quilt is 85½ × 97½ inches
Finished block is 12 inches square

Fabrics and Supplies

✓ 2¾ yards of subtle beige check for the blocks, inner border, and binding

✓ 1¼ yards of a single dark brown plaid for the blocks and pieced border

✓ ¼ yard *each* of 28 different light plaid fabrics for the blocks and pieced border. These may be either regular (9 × 44-inch) or fat (18 × 22-inch) quarters

✓ Scraps (approximately 10 × 18 inches *each*) of 29 different dark plaid fabrics for the blocks and pieced border

✓ 3 yards of 90-inch-wide muslin or 6 yards of 45-inch-wide muslin for the quilt back

✓ Queen-size quilt batting (90 × 108 inches)

✓ Rotary cutter, ruler, and mat

Cutting

The instructions for this quilt are written for quick-cutting the blocks and borders using a rotary cutter and ruler. Quick-piecing methods are included where applicable. Note that for some of the pieces, the quick-cutting method may result in leftovers. All measurements include ¼-inch seam allowances. Measurements for the borders are longer than needed. Trim them to the exact length when they are added to the quilt top. Cut pieces in the following sequence.

From the beige check, cut:
• Nine 2 × 44-inch strips for binding

• Two 9 × 74-inch inner border strips

• Two 9 × 80-inch inner border strips

• Two 6⅞-inch squares. Cut these squares in half diagonally to make 4 D triangles.

• Two 5⅛-inch squares. Cut these squares in half diagonally to make 4 C triangles.

• Two 3⅞-inch squares. Cut these squares in half diagonally to make 4 B triangles

• One 2⅝ × 11-inch strip. Cut this strip into 2⅝-inch squares to make a total of 4 A squares.

From the dark brown plaid, cut:
• One 4¾-inch strip on the lengthwise grain. Cut this strip into 4¾-inch E squares. You will need a total of 4 E squares.

• Fourteen 2⅝-inch strips on the cross grain of the fabric. Cut these strips into 2⅝ × 17-inch strips. You will need a total of 28 of these strips.

• One 6⅞-inch square. Cut this square in half diagonally to make 2 D triangles.

• One 5⅛-inch square. Cut this square in half diagonally to make 2 C triangles.

• One 3⅞-inch square. Cut this square in half diagonally to make 2 B triangles.

• One 2⅝ × 6-inch strip

From each of the light plaid fabrics, cut:
NOTE: If you are cutting from a regular quarter yard of fabric, cut in the order shown. If you are cutting from a fat quarter, cut the longest strip first.

• One 6⅞-inch square. Cut this square in half diagonally to make 2 D triangles.

• One 5⅛-inch square. Cut this square in half diagonally to make 2 C triangles.

• One 3⅞-inch square. Cut this square in half diagonally to make 2 B triangles.

• One 2⅝ × 17-inch strip

• One 2⅝ × 6-inch strip

From each of the 29 dark plaid scraps, cut:
• One 6⅞-inch square. Cut this square in half diagonally to make 2 D triangles.

• One 5⅛-inch square. Cut this square in half diagonally to make 2 C triangles.

• One 3⅞-inch square. Cut this square in half diagonally to make 2 B triangles.

• One 2⅝ × 6-inch strip

Piecing the Blocks

This quilt requires a total of 30 pieced blocks as shown in the **Block Diagram.** Each block includes one light plaid and one dark plaid fabric. Referring to the photograph on page 97, note that two of the blocks use the beige check as the light fabric for pieces A, B, C, and D.

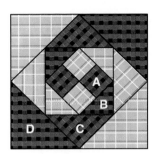

Block Diagram

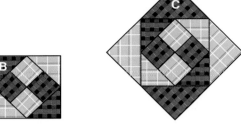

Diagram 2   **Diagram 3**

1. Referring to **Diagram 1,** sew two contrasting (light/dark) $2\frac{5}{8} \times 6$-inch strips along the long edge. Press the seam allowance toward the darker fabric.

$2\frac{5}{8}"$

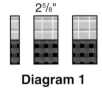

Diagram 1

2. Cut the newly created light/dark strip into two $2\frac{5}{8}$-inch "slices," as shown in **Diagram 1.**

3. Pair the "slices" as shown in the **Four Patch Diagram,** taking care to pin carefully. Because the seam allowances are pressed in opposite directions, the seams will "nest" nicely for a clean match. After stitching, press the seam allowance to one side.

Four Patch Diagram

4. Using the same light and dark plaids, sew a light B triangle to opposite sides of the four patch, as shown in **Diagram 2.** Then sew a dark B triangle to each of the remaining sides, as shown. Press the seam allowances away from the center of the block.

5. Again using the same light and dark plaids, sew a light C triangle to opposite sides of the block, as shown in **Diagram 3.** Sew a dark C triangle to each of the remaining sides, as shown. Press the seam allowances away from the center of the block.

6. Continuing with the same lights and darks, sew a light D triangle to opposite sides of the block, as shown in **Diagram 4.** Sew a dark D triangle to each of the remaining sides, as shown, to complete the block. Press the seam allowances away from the center of the block.

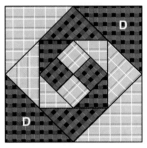

Diagram 4

Assembling the Quilt Top

1. Lay out the blocks in six horizontal rows of five blocks each, referring to the **Quilt Diagram** on page 100 for proper positioning. Note that the lights and darks in each block are rotated in groups of four, as shown in **Diagram 5.** Also note that the blocks containing the beige border fabric are positioned in the upper and lower left corners. They will appear to "float" when the inner borders are attached.

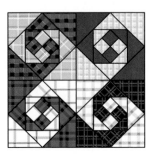

Diagram 5

Quilt Diagram

2. Sew the five blocks in each horizontal row together, pressing the seam allowances between blocks in opposite directions from row to row.

3. Sew the six rows of blocks together, carefully aligning the seams. Press the seam allowances toward the top edge of the quilt top.

Assembling and Attaching the Inner Border

1. Sew the remaining dark D triangles in "nonmatching" pairs along a short side, as

shown in **Diagram 6.** Make a total of five D triangle-pieced units. Press the seam allowances under on the two short sides and prepare them for appliqué by basting them in place if you wish.

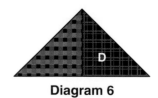

Diagram 6

2. Take the lengthwise measurement of the quilt top. Trim the 9 × 74-inch beige check inner border strips to this measurement and crease them at the midpoints. Match the midpoint of one trimmed border strip with the midpoint of the left side of the quilt top. Pin or baste one of the five D triangle-pieced units in place on the border strip as indicated in the **Quilt Diagram,** aligning the raw edges. With right sides together, pin the border to the quilt, taking care to match the midpoints and appropriate seams. Stitch the border to the quilt top. The raw edge of the D triangle-pieced unit will be caught and hidden in the seam.

3. Repeat the process, using the remaining 9 × 74-inch beige border and two D triangle-pieced units on the right side of the quilt top. Refer to the **Quilt Diagram** for placement.

4. Take the crosswise measurement of the quilt top and trim the 9 × 80-inch borders to this measurement. Position one of the remaining D triangle-pieced units on each border, referring to the **Quilt Diagram** for placement. Sew these borders to the top and bottom of the quilt, following the procedure in Step 2.

5. Appliqué the short sides of the D triangle units to each border, using a blind hem stitch and thread to match the triangles. For more information about hand appliqué, see page 157.

Assembling and Attaching the Outer Border

The outer border requires a total of 78 four-patch units. The consistent fabric in each is the dark brown plaid.

1. Pair a $2\frac{5}{8}$ × 17-inch dark brown plaid strip with a light plaid strip of matching size. Sew them together lengthwise, taking care to maintain a consistent $\frac{1}{4}$-inch seam. Press the seam allowance toward the dark fabric. Make a total of 28 light/dark brown strips.

2. Cut each light/dark strip into six $2\frac{5}{8}$-inch "slices" and sew together three four patch units from each set of slices. There will be a total of 84

four patch units, giving you a few extra units to play with!

3. Join the four patch units into two border strips of 18 units each. Mix the units randomly, so that like four patches do not lie side by side. Make two additional border strips of 21 units each.

Tip: *The pieced borders will be more accurate if you stitch the four patch units together in groups of three, then six, rather than building one long, continuous chain of units.* ★

4. Mark the midpoint of each pieced border strip with a pin. Matching edges and midpoints with the beige inner border, sew an 18-unit border strip to the top and bottom of the quilt top. You may stretch or ease the pieced border slightly, or if the adjustment is too great, take deeper (or narrower) seams in a few of the four patch units to make up the difference.

5. Sew an E square to each end of the remaining (21-unit) border strips and sew these borders to the left and right sides of the quilt top.

Quilting and Finishing

1. Mark quilting designs as desired. The quilt shown is quilted in a diagonal grid that extends into the beige inner border. To mark the lines of this grid, draw lines outward from the center of a block and simply extend them into the adjacent blocks. The four patch border is quilted in the ditch.

2. Layer the quilt backing, batting and quilt top; baste. Trim the backing and batting to approximately 3 inches beyond all sides of the quilt top. Quilt all marked designs.

3. Sew the 2 × 44-inch beige strips together to make approximately 375 inches of double-fold binding.

4. Sew the binding to the quilt top. Trim the excess batting and backing, and hand finish the binding on the back of the quilt. For more instructions on making and attaching binding, see page 164.

Homespun Baskets

Quiltmaker: Ina Sutton

If you've been wanting to experiment with appliqué, Ina's country basket quilt is the perfect chance to try out various techniques. Hand appliqué is used for the basket handles, and machine satin stitching creates a folk art look in the hearts, bows, and flowers. The bow and flower centers are padded slightly to add dimension to this charming wall quilt.

Skill Level: Intermediate

Size: Finished quilt is 36 inches square

Fabrics and Supplies

- ✓ ¾ yard of ecru print fabric for the background
- ✓ ½ yard of red and black plaid fabric for the outer borders
- ✓ ¼ yard of red striped fabric for the inner borders
- ✓ 12-inch square *each* of nine plaid or striped fabrics for the baskets, bows, flowers, and hearts
- ✓ 4-inch square *each* of two green print fabrics for leaf appliqués
- ✓ Paper-backed fusible webbing for the appliqués
- ✓ 1¼ yards of fabric for the quilt back
- ✓ ⅜ yard of black solid fabric for binding
- ✓ Crib-size quilt batting (45 × 60 inches)
- ✓ Template plastic
- ✓ Pencil or removable fabric marker for marking handle appliqué guidelines

Cutting

All measurements, except for the appliqué pieces, include ¼-inch seam allowances. Measurements for the sashing strips and borders are longer than needed; trim them to the exact length when they are added to the quilt top. The basket handle background strip will be cut to the exact length after the appliqué is completed. Use the pattern pieces on page 106 to make templates for the bow, heart, flower, center circles, and leaf appliqués. Seam allowances for the appliqué pattern pieces are added when cutting the pieces out of the fabric.

From the ecru print fabric, cut:
- Three 4½ × 30-inch strips for the basket handle backgrounds
- Six 1½ × 30-inch strips for the sashing strips and side borders
- Eighteen 1½-inch B squares

- Six 3½-inch C squares
- Six 1½ × 3½-inch D rectangles
- Six 1½ × 3-inch E rectangles
- Six 1¼ × 1½-inch G rectangles

From each of the nine striped or plaid fabrics, cut:
- One 3½ × 6½-inch A rectangle
- One 1½ × 7-inch bias F strip
- One 1⅜ × 12-inch bias handle

From the red striped fabric, cut:
- Four 1½ × 34-inch strips for the inner borders

From the red and black plaid homespun fabric, cut:
- Four 3¼ × 40-inch strips for the outer borders

From the remaining scraps of homespun fabrics, cut:
- 3 flowers
- 3 hearts
- 3 bows
- 6 center circles

From one green print fabric, cut:
- 4 leaves

From the other green print fabric, cut:
- 2 leaves

Piecing the Basket Bases

1. Pin a B square to each lower corner of an A rectangle, with right sides together and raw edges aligned. Sew diagonally from corner to corner of the B squares, as shown in **Diagram 1.**

Diagram 1

2. Trim the seams to ¼ inch, as shown in **Diagram 2.** Repeat for the remaining A rectangles.

Diagram 2

3. Press the seam allowances toward the B triangles, completing the basket bases, as shown in **Diagram 3.**

Basket Base
Diagram 3

4. Lay the basket bases out in a row of three baskets. Sew an ecru C square between the basket bases and an ecru D rectangle at each side, as shown in **Diagram 4.** Press the seams toward the basket bases. Repeat for the remaining two rows of basket bases, using the photograph on page 102 as a guide to color placement, or arranging the baskets in a way that pleases you.

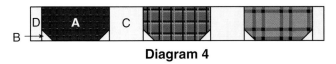

Diagram 4

5. Lay out a row of bias F strips above the row of basket bases, matching the fabrics in the basket bases. Sew an ecru E rectangle between each bias F strip and an ecru G rectangle at each end, as shown in **Diagram 5.** Press the seams toward the F strips.

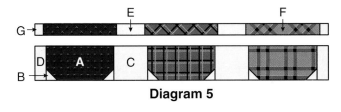

Diagram 5

Appliquéing the Handles

1. Using the pattern on page 106, make a handle placement template. Center the handle placement template on the midpoint of an ecru basket handle background strip. Using a pencil or removable fabric marker, lightly mark the guideline on the front of the strip. Mark another handle guideline 3 inches on either side of the center guideline, as shown in **Diagram 6.** Repeat for the other two basket handle background strips.

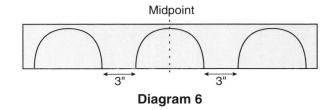

Midpoint

3" 3"

Diagram 6

2. Fold and press the raw edges of the 1⅜-inch bias handle strip in so that they meet at the center of the strip, creating a handle that is approximately ½ inch wide. Matching the fabric of each handle to the appropriate basket, thread baste the handles along the curves on the basket handle background strips. Note that these bias handles are slightly longer than needed. The ends will extend beyond the edge of the background strip.

3. Appliqué the inner curves of each handle first, then the outer curves, so that the handles lie flat. Remove the basting threads and trim the ends of the handles even with the ecru background strip. Cut the background strip to 26½ inches long. There should be approximately 1½ inches beyond the edge of each handle.

4. Sew the handle rows to the basket rows, as shown in **Diagram 7,** making sure that the handles are spaced evenly above the basket bases. Press the seams toward the F strips.

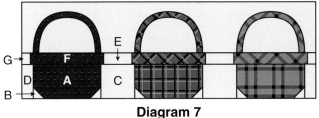

Diagram 7

Assembling the Quilt Top

1. Measure the length of the basket rows. Trim four 1½ × 30-inch ecru sashing strips to this measurement. Referring to the **Quilt Diagram,** lay out the rows of baskets in horizontal rows with a sashing strip between each row, and at the top and bottom. Sew the basket rows and sashing strips together and press the seams toward the sashing strips.

2. Measure the length of the quilt top. Trim two ecru sashing strips to this measurement.

Referring to the **Quilt Diagram,** sew sashing strips to the side edges of the quilt top, creating side borders. Press the seams toward the side borders.

3. Measure the width of the quilt top. Trim the top and bottom striped homespun inner borders to this measurement and sew them to the top and bottom of the quilt top. Press the seams toward the borders.

4. Measure the length of the quilt top, including the borders you just added. Trim the remaining two inner border strips to this measurement and sew them to the side edges of the quilt top. Press the seams toward the borders.

5. In the same manner, add the red and black plaid outer borders, completing the quilt top, as shown in the **Quilt Diagram.**

Appliquéing the Flowers, Bows, and Leaves

1. Follow the directions on page 158 for using fusible webbing to prepare, cut out, position, and fuse the hearts and bows for machine appliqué. Refer to the photograph on page 102 for placement. Do not fuse the bow center circles. Match the top thread in the sewing machine to the appliqué pieces and machine satin stitch the bows and hearts in place. For more information on machine satin stitch appliqué, see page 158.

2. In the same manner, appliqué the leaves and overlap them with the flowers, as shown in the photograph.

3. Appliqué the centers on the bows and the flowers using a blind stitch, padding each piece lightly with a small amount of batting as you continue to sew.

Quilting and Finishing

1. Mark quilting designs. The quilt in the photo is quilted in the ditch along the sashing strips and borders. There is also outline quilting around each basket and appliqué shape. The basket bases are quilted in a grid of lines approximately 1 inch apart, using the lines in the plaid

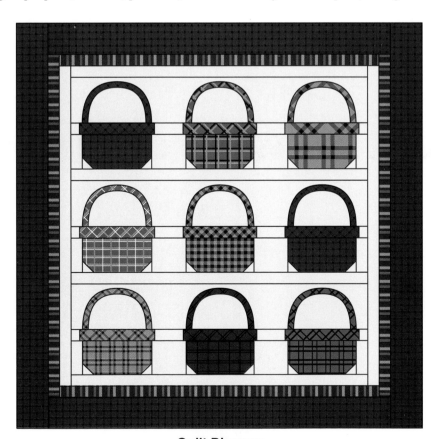

Quilt Diagram

fabrics as a guide. There is a ½-inch diagonal grid inside each basket handle and three rows of echo quilting ½ inch apart between the basket handles. Between each basket base, a heart is marked with the heart appliqué template, and in the outer border, the same heart template is used to create a pattern of interlocking hearts.

2. Layer the quilt back, batting, and quilt top; baste. Trim the quilt back and batting to approximately 3 inches larger than the quilt top.

3. Quilt all marked designs, and add any additional quilting as desired.

4. From the black solid fabric, make approximately 154 inches of double-fold binding. See page 164 for instructions on making and attaching binding.

5. Sew the binding to the quilt top. Trim the excess batting and backing, and hand stitch the binding to the back of the quilt. Refer to page 167 for directions on adding a hanging sleeve.

"PENNY-WISE" APPLIQUÉ

To make quick-and-easy, perfectly shaped centers for the bows and hearts in Homespun Baskets, try this trick. Trace around a penny on the wrong side of the fabric. Run a basting thread approximately ⅛ inch outside the perimeter of the drawn circle, and cut it out approximately ⅛ inch beyond the basting thread. Position a penny on the drawn circle and pull on the basting thread, gathering the fabric over the penny. Tighten and knot the thread to secure the gathers. Press the fabric circle from the back, using spray starch if desired. After letting the penny cool, remove both the gathering thread and the penny. Finger press the gathered fabric flat and pin the circle in place on a bow or flower. Appliqué it by hand with a blind stitch. To pad the circle, just insert a penny-size piece of batting underneath it as you stitch it in place. ◆

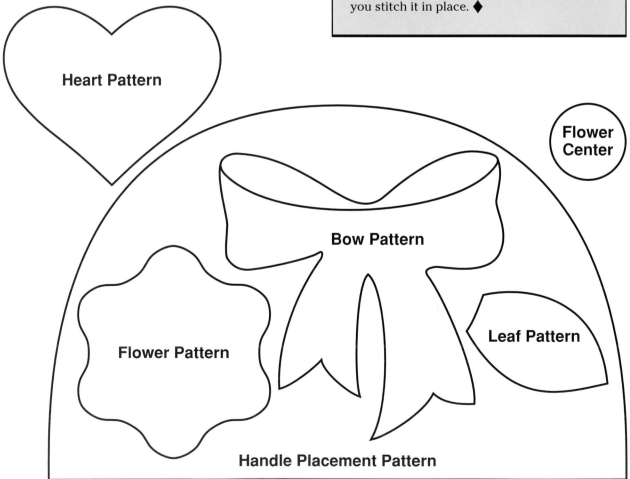

Heart Pattern

Flower Center

Bow Pattern

Leaf Pattern

Flower Pattern

Handle Placement Pattern

Ocean and Skies

Quiltmaker: Joan Dyer

Joan's soothing quilt features several surprises, including a variety of gorgeous batiks, hand-dyed fabrics, and other specialty prints, as well as a very unusual border treatment. She even included a final design twist in the form of a randomly pieced plaid binding.

107

Skill Level: Intermediate

Size: Finished quilt is 40 × 56 inches
Finished block is 8 inches square

Fabrics and Supplies

This quilt contains a wide variety of blue and beige stripes and plaids in light, medium, and dark color values, along with specialty prints such as batiks and hand-dyed fabrics. There is also a "surprise" red that adds a real spark of excitement to the other colors in the quilt. Red is always a dynamic touch in a combination of cool blues, but choose any color you like to accent your fabric choices. The yardages listed are generous, to enable you to work either with scraps or with larger pieces of fabric.

- ✓ Scraps of swirly prints in dark, medium, and light values, *totaling* ¾ yard for the block center squares. Each scrap must be at least 4½ inches square
- ✓ Scraps *totaling* 3 yards of light, medium, and dark blue striped and plaid fabrics for the blocks and binding
- ✓ Scraps *totaling* ¾ yard of light and medium beige striped and plaid fabrics for the blocks
- ✓ Scraps *totaling* ¼ yard of bright red prints for the blocks and binding
- ✓ 1¾ yards of fabric for the quilt back
- ✓ Crib-size batting (45 × 60 inches)
- ✓ Rotary cutter, ruler, and mat
- ✓ Template material

Cutting

These instructions are for cutting 15 center blocks, 16 border blocks, and 4 corner blocks. If you wish to add a "suprise" red square to one of the corners, as in the quilt shown, refer to the "Creative Border Twist" tip on page 111 for how to construct a unique two-block border unit. The A and B triangles are cut with a rotary cutter and ruler. These measurements include ¼-inch seam allowances. Note that quick cutting will yield some leftover triangles. Pieces C and D are cut using the templates on page 111. If you prefer to work entirely with templates, or if you are working with small scraps, the templates for each of the pieces in this quilt are given on page 111.

Before you start to cut pieces and plan color value placements, note that each of the 15 Center blocks requires four of the same dark A triangles and eight of the same light or medium A triangles. Also, the fabrics placed along the edges of this quilt are darker in value than those in the rest of the quilt. Use the quilt photograph on page 107 for color guidance, or if you have a large scrap bag, you may enjoy experimenting to create a different color scheme of your own.

For the Center Blocks
From the swirly print fabrics, cut:
- Fifteen 4½-inch center squares

From various blue and beige striped and plaid fabrics, cut:
- Forty-five 5¼-inch squares. Cut these squares diagonally in both directions to make 180 A triangles.

From the red print fabrics, cut:
- 1 C triangle

For the Border Blocks
From the swirly print fabrics, cut:
- Fifteen 4½-inch center squares

From various blue and beige striped and plaid fabrics, cut:
- Forty 5¼-inch squares. Cut these squares diagonally in both directions to make 160 A triangles.
- Fifteen 4½-inch squares. Cut these squares in half diagonally in both directions to make 60 B triangles.

From the red print fabrics, cut:
- 2 C triangles

For the Corner Blocks
From the swirly print fabrics, cut:
- Four 4½-inch center squares

From the blue and beige striped and plaid fabrics, cut:
- Ten 5¼-inch squares. Cut these squares in half diagonally in both directions to make 40 A triangles.
- Eight 3¾-inch squares. Cut these squares in half diagonally to make 16 B triangles.

From the red print fabrics, cut:
- One 3½-inch D square

Piecing the Center Blocks

1. Sew four matching striped or plaid dark A triangles to each side of a center fabric square, as shown in **Diagram 1.** Press the seams toward the triangles.

Center Block

Diagram 1

2. For the following pairs of A triangles, select a light or medium striped or plaid fabric that contrasts with the dark A triangle fabric used in Step 1. Sew two matching striped or plaid A triangles together, creating a large outer A/A unit, as shown in **Diagram 1.** Repeat to make three more A/A units and sew them to the corners of the block. Press the seams toward the A/A units.

3. Make 15 of these center blocks. One of the center blocks in the quilt shown has a surprise red C triangle as an accent at one of the corners.

Making the Border Blocks

The border blocks are similar to the center blocks, with only a few changes in color value.

1. Referring to **Diagram 2,** sew matching light or medium plaid or striped A triangles to three sides of the center square, as shown. Sew a very dark plaid or striped A triangle to the remaining side of the center square. This A triangle will be placed at the outer edge of the quilt, creating the darker effect of the border. Press the seam allowances away from the center of the block.

2. Referring to **Diagram 3,** sew together two matching light or medium A triangles to form an A/A unit, as shown. Repeat to form another of these A/A units in the same fabric. Sew the matching A/A units to two sides of the center square, as shown.

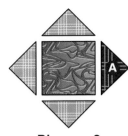 

Diagram 2   **Diagram 3**

3. Referring to **Diagram 4,** sew together two B triangles, one that matches the previously attached A/A units, and the other in a slightly darker value fabric to make a B/B unit. Then sew an A triangle in the same slightly darker value fabric to the B/B unit, as shown. Repeat to create another A/B/B unit, as shown, and sew them to the sides of the center square. This completes the border block. This side of the border block will be placed along the outer edge of the quilt, creating the darker effect of the border. Press the seam allowances away from the center of the border block.

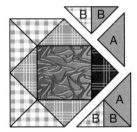

Border Block

Diagram 4

4. Make 16 border blocks. In the quilt shown, 2 of the border blocks include a red C triangle at one corner of the block. If you've chosen a different "surprise" fabric, substitute it in these places.

Making the Corner Blocks

Referring to **Diagram 5** on page 110 for an example of a corner block and the quilt photograph on page 107 for further guidance in placing color values, make four corner blocks. As you make the corner blocks, choose from light, medium, or dark values, as long as the overall effect of the outer border is slightly darker in value than the center of the quilt. The corner blocks are assembled in the same way as the border blocks.

Corner Block

Diagram 5

Assembling the Quilt Top

1. Referring to the **Quilt Diagram** and the photograph on page 107 for placement, lay out the center blocks, border blocks, and corner blocks.

2. Sew the quilt top together into five vertical rows, pressing the seam allowances in opposite directions between the blocks.

3. Sew the five vertical rows together, completing the quilt top. Press the seam allowances in alternating directions between the rows.

Quilting and Finishing

1. Mark quilting designs as desired. The quilt shown is quilted in the ditch around each piece.

2. Layer the quilt top, batting, and backing; baste. Trim the quilt back and batting so they are approximately 3 inches larger than the quilt top on all sides.

3. Quilt all marked designs, adding additional quilting as desired.

4. From scrap fabrics, cut strips 2½ inches wide on the crosswise grain of the fabric. Also cut several short strips of different plaids that

Quilt Diagram

are 2½ inches wide, varying in length from 3 to 5 inches. Place short plaid strips between longer strips and sew the pieces together with diagonal seams to create approximately 220 inches of decorative binding. Press these seams open to reduce bulk in the binding.

5. Attach the binding to the quilt top. Trim the excess batting and back and turn the binding to the back. Hand finish with an invisible stitch. For more information on making and attaching binding, see page 164.

6. To make a hanging sleeve for displaying the quilt, hem the short ends of an 8½ × 40-inch strip of fabric and sew it into a tube along the long edges. Hand sew the sleeve to the upper back edge of the quilt.

A CREATIVE BORDER TWIST

Joan added a single red square as a delightful "surprise" accent to one corner of her quilt. If you'd like to achieve the same effect in your own quilt, just substitute a bright red (or any other vibrant color you like) D square in place of two A triangles between one border block and one corner block. Construct this border unit in the manner shown in the **Border Unit Diagram** in order to insert the D square easily. ◆

Border Unit Diagram

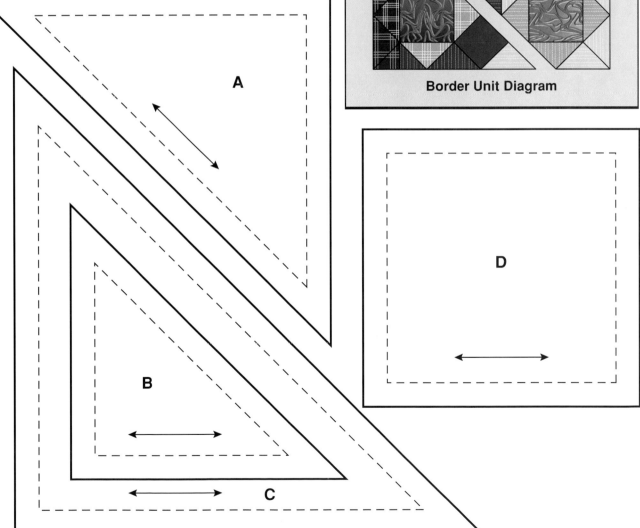

Country Wedding Ring

Quiltmaker: Susan Stein

Plaids and stripes combine beautifully in this dramatic wall quilt. The richness of Susan's quilt is enhanced by the combination of a deep dark background print with Wedding Rings in much lighter color values. Eight different plaids form the Wedding Rings, and each ring is separated by an eye-catching hint of the same black and beige plaid she chose for the binding.

Skill Level: Intermediate

Size: Finished quilt is 42 × 52 inches

Fabrics and Supplies

- ✓ 1½ yards of medium red striped fabric for the background in the rings
- ✓ 1½ yards of red print for the quilt background
- ✓ ¼ yard *each* of four different light plaid fabrics for the rings
- ✓ ¼ yard *each* of two different medium plaid fabrics for the rings
- ✓ ¼ yard *each* of two different dark plaid fabrics for the rings
- ✓ ½ yard of a black/beige plaid fabric for the rings and binding
- ✓ 1⅝ yards of fabric for the quilt back
- ✓ Crib-size batting (45 × 60 inches)
- ✓ Template material

Cutting

Pattern pieces A through E are provided on page 116. The patterns include ¼-inch seam allowances. As you decide which plaid or striped fabric to cut for each of the pieces, refer to the quilt photograph for fabric placement.

From the medium red striped fabric, cut:
- 16 B pieces on the lengthwise grain of the fabric
- 15 B pieces on the crosswise grain of the fabric
- 12 A pieces

From light plaid fabrics, cut:
- A *total* of 124 C pieces: 62 from one plaid fabric and 62 from another plaid fabric
- 62 D pieces

From medium plaid fabrics, cut:
- 62 D reverse pieces
- 62 C pieces
- 30 E pieces

From dark plaid fabrics, cut:
- 62 C pieces

From the black/beige plaid fabric, cut:
- 32 E pieces

Piecing the Wedding Rings

1. Referring to **Diagram 1,** sew together a medium plaid C piece, a light plaid C, a dark plaid C, and a light plaid C, as shown. Add a medium D reverse piece to one end and a light D piece to the other end, as shown. Press the seam allowances to one side. Make a total of 62 of these pieced arcs.

2. Referring to **Diagram 2,** sew a black/beige plaid E piece to each end of 16 of these pieced arcs, as shown. Sew a medium plaid E piece to each end of 15 of the pieced arcs, as shown. Press the seam allowances toward the arc centers.

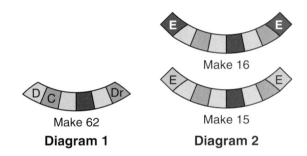

Make 16

Make 62
Diagram 1

Make 15
Diagram 2

3. Before proceeding to assemble the wedding rings, check to make sure that you have a total of 16 long pieced arcs with black/beige plaid E pieces at each end, 15 long pieced arcs with medium plaid E pieces at each end, and 31 remaining short pieced arcs with no E pieces at either end.

4. Referring to **Diagram 3,** sew a short pieced arc to one side of a B piece, placing the striped fabric in the B piece, as shown. Press the seam allowance toward the B piece. Sew a long pieced arc with medium plaid E pieces at the ends to the other side of this B piece, as shown. Repeat to make a total of 15 of these pieced arc units. For more information on sewing curved seams, see page 59.

Make 15

Diagram 3

5. Referring to **Diagram 4,** make 16 more pieced arc units, placing the medium red striped fabric in the B pieces, as shown, and using the 16 long pieced arcs that have black/beige plaid E pieces at the ends, as shown.

Make 16
Diagram 4

6. Referring to **Diagram 5,** sew four of the pieced arc units from step 5 together with three medium red striped A pieces, forming a row, as shown. Begin and end each of these seams ¼ inch in from the edges of each D and D reverse piece, as indicated by the dots in the diagram. Press the seam allowances toward the A pieces. Make four of these rows.

7. Referring to **Diagram 6,** sew the three pieced arc units that have medium plaid E pieces at the ends at the bottom of one row. Begin and end each of these seams where the E pieces meet the D and D reverse pieces, as indicated by the dots in the diagram. Press the seam allowances toward the A pieces.

8. Referring to **Diagram 7,** sew the seams of the E pieces on adjoining sides of each A piece, as shown. Press these seam allowances in opposite directions. This completes the bottom row of Wedding Rings.

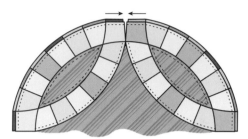

Diagram 7

9. Referring to the **Quilt Diagram,** sew pieced arc units between the remaining rows of Wedding Rings, beginning and ending each of these in the same manner as before. Press the seam allowances toward the A pieces. This allows the E pieces to remain unstitched.

10. Referring to **Diagram 7,** complete the seams at each juncture where two E pieces come together on adjoining sides of an A piece, as shown. Press these seam allowances in opposite directions.

11. Referring to **Diagram 8,** complete the seams at each juncture where four E pieces come together between the Wedding Rings, as shown. Press these seam allowances to one side of the unit.

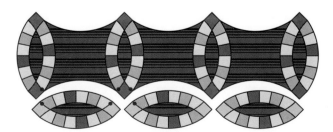

Make 4 rows
Diagram 5

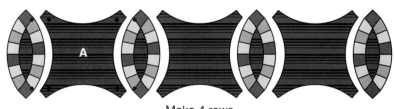

Diagram 6

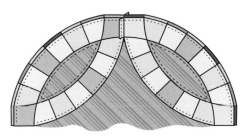

Diagram 8

12. Referring to the **Quilt Diagram,** place the joined Wedding Rings on the dark red print background fabric and appliqué them in place by hand or machine. Use whichever technique you like best. For information on hand and machine appliqué, see pages 157–159.

13. After all of the Wedding Rings have been appliquéd, trim the excess background fabric from behind the Wedding Rings to ¼ inch from the appliquéd stitching. Trimming the excess will allow you to quilt through fewer layers of fabric.

Quilting and Finishing

1. Mark quilting designs as desired. The quilt shown has a spider web quilted in the center of each ring and random leaves quilted between the arcs and around the outer edges of the quilt. It is also quilted in the ditch around the rings, with three added concentric rows of quilting approximately ¼ inch apart around the rings.

2. Layer the quilt top, batting, and back; baste. Trim the back and batting to approximately 3 inches larger than the quilt top on all sides. Quilt all marked quilting designs.

3. From the binding fabric, make approximately 300 inches of double-fold, straight-grain binding. For instructions on making and attaching binding, see page 164.

4. Sew the binding to the quilt top. Trim the excess batting and backing. Using thread to match the binding, hand finish the binding with an invisible stitch on the back of the quilt.

Quilt Diagram

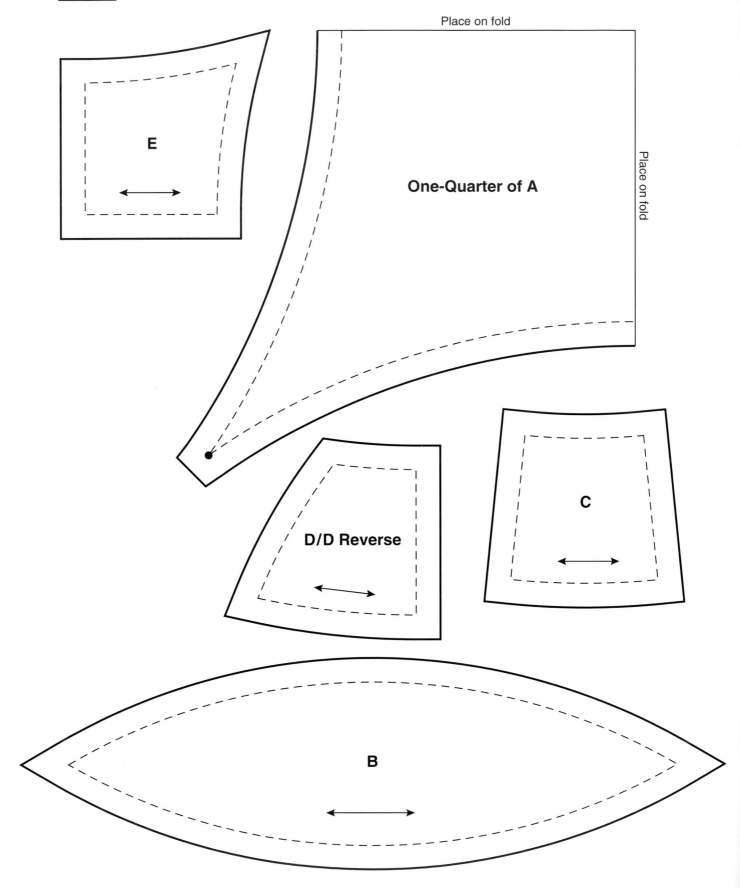

Place on fold

E

One-Quarter of A

Place on fold

D/D Reverse

C

B

Plaid Folk Hearts

Quiltmaker: Roberta Horton

Roberta chose homespun plaid fabrics to make hearts that look as if they were taken from old shirts. Buttons in various shapes and sizes add a whimsical touch. The irregular shapes and unfinished edges of her raw-edge appliqué technique create a feeling of exuberance in this delightfully free-spirited folk art quilt. You can give your quilt the same exuberance by cutting freeform hearts from your favorite stripes, plaids, and shirting reproduction fabrics.

Skill Level: Easy

Size: Finished quilt is approximately 24 inches × 28½ inches
Finished block is approximately 4½ inches square

Fabrics and Supplies

✓ Approximately ½ yard *total* of assorted plaid homespun fabrics for the borders

✓ Scraps (*each* approximately 6 inches square) of 40 different homespun fabrics for the blocks and hearts

✓ 1 yard of green plaid homespun fabric for the quilt back

✓ ¼ yard of red plaid homespun fabric for the binding

✓ Crib-size quilt batting (45 × 60 inches)

✓ 1 yard of lightweight Tear-Away fabric stabilizer

✓ Assorted buttons and ribbons for embellishing the hearts

✓ 1 skein of embroidery floss for tying the quilt

Cutting

Except for the appliqués, all measurements include ¼-inch seam allowances. Measurements for the borders are slightly longer than needed; trim them to the exact length when they are added to the quilt top.

From the assorted plaid homespun fabrics, cut:
• Enough 3½-inch-wide strips to piece together four 3½ × 34-inch strips for borders

From the homespun fabric scraps, cut:
• Twenty 5-inch squares for blocks

• 20 heart shapes freehand; see "Hey, I Can Do This!" for information on freehand cutting techniques. **NOTE:** It's a good idea to cut more than 20 hearts, so you can experiment with various color and fabric combinations.

• From the Tear-Away fabric stabilizer, cut twenty 5-inch squares

Appliquéing the Hearts

1. Pin or baste a square of Tear-Away under each 5-inch square of fabric to stabilize it and pin a heart to each block. Refer to the photograph on page 117 for color placement or experiment with your own fabrics on a design surface until you have combinations that please you. Using dark thread or any contrasting color, straight stitch each heart to the block by machine, approximately ¼ inch in from the edge. If the lines of stitching appear uneven, it will only add to the charm of the quilt.

2. Using a combination of straight and zigzag stitches, sew around each heart again. Use a playful approach to these lines, remembering that irregular lines of stitching enhance the free-spirited style of the quilt. You can also use more than one color of thread on each heart; refer to the photograph for more decorative stitching ideas. Carefully remove the Tear-Away from each block after the lines of stitching are complete.

Assembling the Quilt Top

1. Lay out the blocks in five horizontal rows with four blocks in each row. Refer to the photograph on page 117 for color placement or play with different color combinations of your own until you find an arrangement that pleases you.

2. Sew the blocks together in rows, as shown in **Diagram 1.** Press the seams of alternate rows in opposite directions.

Diagram 1

3. Referring to **Diagram 1,** sew the rows together and press the seams in opposite directions.

4. Measure the width of the quilt top and trim the top and bottom border strips to this measurement. Referring to the **Quilt Diagram,** the borders to the top and bottom of the quilt top. Press the seams toward the borders.

5. Measure the length of the quilt top, including borders you just added, and trim the side border strips to this measurement. Referring to the **Quilt Diagram,** sew the borders to the sides of the quilt top. Press the seams toward the borders.

Quilt Diagram

Quilting and Finishing

1. Layer the quilt back, batting, and quilt top; baste. Trim the quilt back so that it is approximately 2 inches larger than the quilt top on all sides.

2. Quilt as desired. The quilt shown is machine quilted in the ditch between blocks. The borders are quilted in a zigzag pattern.

3. From the red homespun fabric, make approximately 130 inches of French-fold binding. See page 164 for instructions on making and attaching binding.

4. Sew the binding to the quilt top. Trim the excess batting and backing, and hand finish the binding on the back of the quilt.

5. Embellish the hearts with buttons and ribbons, using the photograph on page 117 as a guide. If you choose to do hand quilting, sew the buttons onto the quilt top before layering it. If you do machine quilting, sew the buttons on with embroidery floss after the quilting is finished. Embroidery floss adds to the primitive look of this quilt, and makes it easy to sew the buttons on. Because floss is made up of six individual strands of thread, you may go through each hole of a button just one time. And for a decorative finish, tie the floss into a knot on the back of the quilt.

HEY, I CAN DO THIS!

This quilt offers a chance to loosen up and take a welcome break from the pressure often involved in working with exact seam allowances and precise points. As you cut out the 20 hearts, have fun and don't worry about making them symmetrical. Fold a 4-inch square of fabric in half, cut out a free-hand heart, and open it up to inspect your results. Then fold another square of fabric in half and cut the next heart a bit differently. For example, you can make it fatter or more pointed, as shown in the diagram. It's important to make them look different from one another, rather than like they've been cut with a cookie cutter or template. As you become braver, try cutting heart shapes from unfolded squares to create an asymmetrical or lopsided look. ◆

HOLIDAYS
and
CELEBRATIONS

Stars, Leaves, and Currants

Quiltmaker: Marge Karavitis

Showcase your hand appliqué and quilting skills in this splendid adaptation of an early twentieth–century beauty. Inspired by a photo in *Treasury of American Quilts,* Marge added her own special touches, including lavishly quilted feathered plumes in the blocks and borders. The vibrant red and green color scheme makes this a perfect Christmas quilt.

Skill Level: Challenging

Size: Finished quilt is 88 inches square
Finished block is 20 inches square

Fabrics and Supplies

- ✓ 7½ yards of unbleached muslin for the background squares, sashes, borders, and binding
- ✓ 2 yards of red solid fabric for the stars, currants, border cable, and other appliqué pieces
- ✓ 2 yards of green solid fabric for the stems, leaves, currants, border cables, and other appliqué pieces
- ✓ ¼ yard of red floral print fabric for the star centers
- ✓ 2⅝ yards of 108-inch-wide unbleached muslin for the quilt back (or 8 yards of 45-inch-wide unbleached muslin)
- ✓ Queen-size quilt batting (90 × 108 inches)
- ✓ Rotary cutter, ruler, and mat
- ✓ Large sheet (20½ inches square) of tracing paper
- ✓ Black permanent marking pen
- ✓ Water-soluble marker or mechanical pencil
- ✓ Template material
- ✓ Thread to match the appliqué pieces

Cutting

Instructions are for quick cutting the background blocks, sashes, and borders with a rotary cutter and ruler. These measurements include ¼-inch seam allowances. Measurements for the borders are slightly longer than needed; trim them to the correct length when adding them to the quilt top.

Make templates for the appliqué shapes, using the appliqué pattern pieces on pages 127–128. Appliqué pattern pieces are given finished size; add the seam allowances when cutting them out of the fabric.

From the unbleached muslin, cut:
- Four 8½ × 90-inch outer border strips
- Four 2½ × 90-inch inner border strips
- Two 4½ × 68½-inch lengthwise sashing strips
- Six 4½ × 20½-inch sashing strips
- Nine 20½-inch squares for the background squares
- If you choose 108-inch-wide muslin for the quilt back, do not cut it. If you use 45-inch wide fabric, cut it into three equal lengths of approximately 45 × 94 inches.
- One 30-inch square for the binding

From the red solid fabric, cut:
- 25 B stars
- 72 E leaves
- 564 D currants
- One 24-inch square. Cut this square into a continuous bias strip approximately ⅞ inch wide; cut this strip into twelve 26-inch segments for the border cables. For more information on making continuous-cut bias strips, see page 164.

From the green solid fabric, cut:
- 36 F leaves
- 36 A leaves
- 49 D currants
- One 27-inch square. Cut this square into a continuous bias strip approximately ⅞ inch wide; cut this strip into thirty-six 8-inch segments for the stems and twelve 26-inch segments for the border cables.

From the red floral print fabric, cut:
- 25 C circles

Appliquéing the Blocks

Each of the nine large blocks in this quilt requires four green A leaves, one red B star, one red floral print C circle, 60 red D currants, one green D currant, eight red E leaves, four green F leaves, and four green stems. Prepare the appliqué shapes according to your preferred method of hand appliqué. For more information on hand appliqué, see page 157. For instructions on making continuous-cut bias strips and tips on using bias presser bars to make perfect bias stems, see page 158. The bias stems and border cables should finish approximately ¼ inch wide.

1. Make a master pattern for positioning the appliqué pieces on the background squares by folding a 20½-inch square of tracing paper in half vertically, horizontally, and diagonally in both directions. Referring to the **Block Diagram** for correct placement of the appliqué shapes, use a pencil to draw the outlines of the finished shapes on the tracing paper and remember that some of the shapes overlap. When you have completed the master pattern, darken the drawn lines with a permanent marking pen and allow the ink to dry before marking appliqué guidelines on the fabric background squares.

Block Diagram

2. Fold a background square in half vertically, horizontally, and diagonally both ways, and crease lightly.

3. Center the background square over the master pattern. Using a water-soluble marking pen or a mechanical pencil, lightly transfer the appliqué guidelines on the master pattern to the background square.

4. Place the green A leaves in position. Pin or baste to secure in place and appliqué them with a blind stitch.

5. Place the green stems in position on the background square, checking to make sure that the red B star and the final red D currant will overlap the raw ends of each stem when they are stitched in place. Pin or baste to secure and appliqué each piece.

6. Layer a red B star, a floral print C circle and a green D currant at the center of the block. Pin or baste to secure and then appliqué them in place.

7. Appliqué 60 red D currants in place on the sides of the four green stems.

8. Appliqué the red E and green F leaves in place, remembering that at the center of each block, the green F leaves overlap the red E leaves, as shown in **Diagram 1.** At the outer corners of each block, the red E leaves stand alone, as shown, and should be appliquéd to a point at the bottom of the leaf.

9. Make a total of nine blocks.

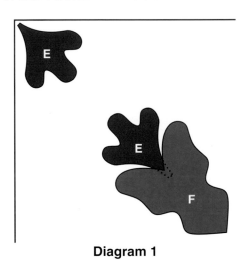

Diagram 1

Assembling the Quilt Top

1. Referring to **Diagram 2,** place the appliquéd blocks in three vertical rows of three blocks each. Insert a 4½ × 20½-inch horizontal sash between each block in each row, as shown. Sew the blocks and sashes together to complete the three vertical rows. Press the seam allowances away from the blocks.

2. Referring to **Diagram 2,** insert a 4½ × 68½-inch sashing strip between each of the three vertical rows of blocks. Sew the rows and long sashing strips together, aligning the blocks horizontally before beginning to sew. Press the seam allowances away from the blocks.

3. Referring to **Diagram 2,** pin or lightly mark the midpoints of each vertical and horizontal sashing strip. These markings, along with the four corners of the quilt top, will help to indicate the correct locations for the border appliqués later.

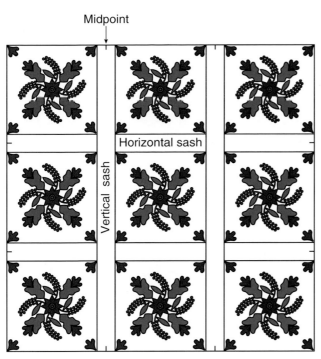

Midpoint

Horizontal sash

Vertical sash

Diagram 2

Appliquéing the Sashing Strips

1. Referring to the **Quilt Diagram** on page 126, place a red B star, a red floral print C circle, and a green D currant at each intersection of the vertical and horizontal sashing strips. Pin or baste to secure in place and appliqué.

2. Referring to the **Quilt Diagram,** alternate a red and a green D currant between the star points on each of the four intersecting sashing strips and appliqué in place.

3. Wait until after you have attached the borders to appliqué the remaining red B stars, red and green border cables, and red and green D currants.

Attaching the Borders

1. Referring to the **Quilt Diagram** on page 126, sew a 2½ × 90-inch and an 8½ × 90-inch border strip together along the long sides to make a single border unit. Press the seam allowance toward the wider border. Make four of these border units.

2. Sew a border unit to each side of the quilt top. Miter each of the corner seams and trim excess fabric as needed. Press the seam allowances away from the quilt top. For more information on mitering corners, see page 160.

Completing the Border Appliqués

1. Referring to the **Border Diagram,** place a red B star, a red floral print C circle and a green D currant at each of the eight previously marked locations as well as in the four corners of the quilt top.

2. Place a red and a green bias strip in the narrow muslin border between each border star, as indicated in the **Border Diagram.** Tuck the raw edges under the red B stars, trimming fabric as necessary from the bias strips. Baste the strips in place and appliqué.

3. Referring to the **Border Diagram,** appliqué the red B stars, red floral print C circles, and green D currants in place.

4. To complete the borders, alternate a red and a green D currant between the appropriate star points, as shown in the **Border Diagram.**

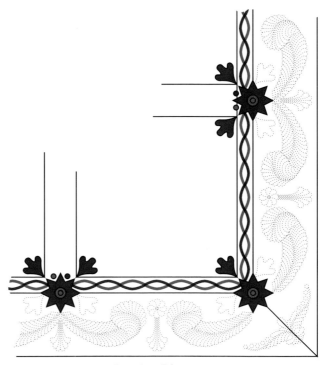

Border Diagram

Quilt Diagram

Quilting and Finishing

1. Mark quilting designs as desired. The quilt shown is quilted in a double outline around each of the appliqué shapes. A quilted feathered plume accents each block, extending into the sashing strip, for which a full-size pattern is given on page 129. This same feathered plume appears in the border, along with the additional quilting motifs shown on pages 128–129. The background of the entire quilt top is quilted in diagonal lines spaced ½ inch apart.

2. If your quilt back is made from 45-inch-wide fabric, trim the selvages from three 44 × 94-inch pieces of muslin and sew them together along the long edges. Press these seams open.

3. Layer the quilt back, batting, and quilt top; baste. Trim the quilt back and batting to approximately 3 inches larger than the quilt top on all sides.

4. Quilt all marked designs. The quilt shown has the quiltmaker's initials and the date quilted in the lower corner.

5. From the binding fabric, make approximately 365 inches of double-fold, continuous bias binding. For more information on making and attaching continuous bias binding, see page 164.

6. Sew the binding to the quilt top. Trim the excess batting and backing, and use matching thread and a blind stitch to hand finish the binding on the back of the quilt.

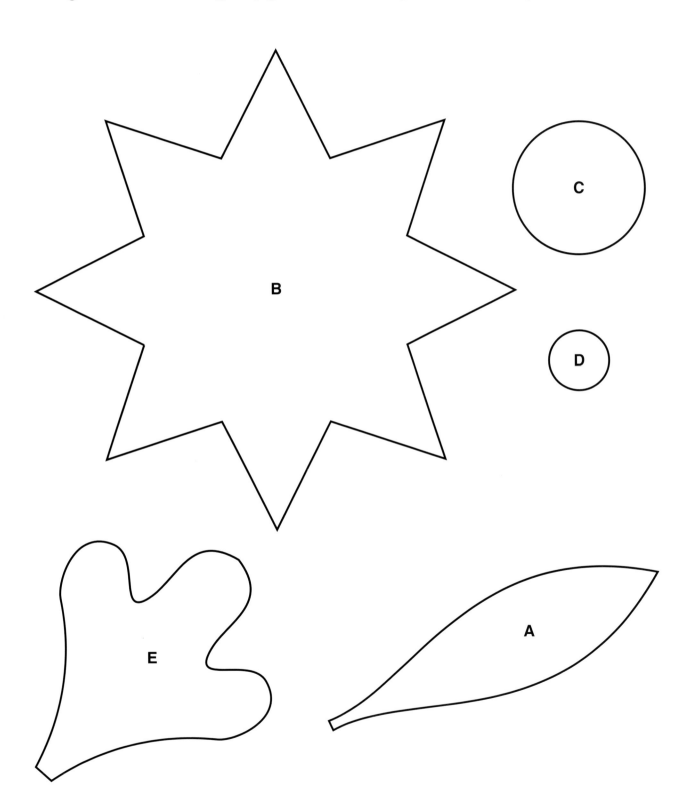

Half-Corner Quilting Pattern

Flip and match for mirror image

F

Tassel Quilting Pattern

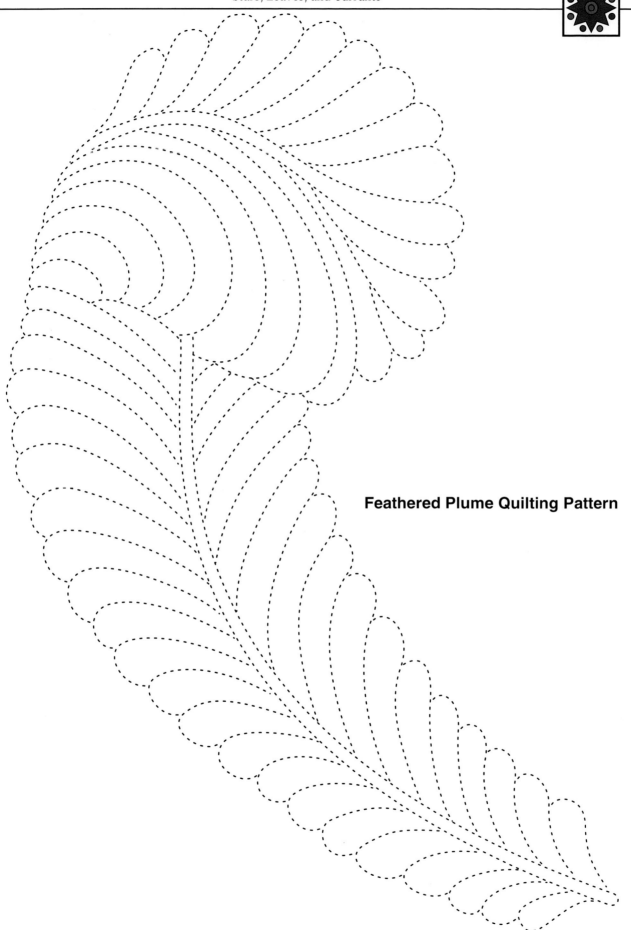

Feathered Plume Quilting Pattern

Christmas Wedding Ring

Quiltmaker: Susan Stein

Colorful Christmas poinsettias bloom at the centers of each ring in this festive table runner. If you've always wanted to try your hand at piecing a traditional Wedding Ring pattern but were afraid to try, this five-block project is a wonderful introduction.

Skill Level: Intermediate

Size: Finished quilt is 18 × 61 inches

Fabrics and Supplies

Yardages listed are generous, although you may need to increase the amount of the focal Christmas print fabric, depending on the type of focal fabric you select and the portions of it you wish to feature at the center of each block.

- ✓ 1 yard of focal fabric for the wedding rings
- ✓ 1 yard of black solid for the background
- ✓ ⅛ yard of light green solid fabric for the blocks
- ✓ ⅛ yard of medium green solid fabric for the blocks
- ✓ ⅛ yard of dark green solid fabric for the blocks
- ✓ ⅛ yard of light red solid fabric for the blocks
- ✓ ½ yard of medium red solid fabric for the blocks and binding
- ✓ ⅛ yard of dark red solid fabric for the blocks
- ✓ ⅛ yard of a small-scale black/red print for the rings
- ✓ ⅛ yard of a dark red print for the rings
- ✓ 1 yard of black solid fabric for the quilt back
- ✓ Twin-size batting (72 × 90 inches)
- ✓ Template material

Cutting

Templates for pattern pieces A through E are provided on page 116. All measurements include ¼-inch seam allowances.

From the focal Christmas print fabric, cut:
- 5 A pieces
- 16 B pieces

From the medium green solid, cut:
- 32 C pieces

From the dark green solid, cut:
- 32 C pieces

From the medium red solid, cut:
- 32 C pieces
- Reserve the remaining fabric for the binding

From the dark red solid, cut:
- 32 C pieces

From the light green solid, cut:
- 32 D reverse pieces

From the light red solid, cut:
- 32 D pieces

From the red/black print, cut:
- 20 E pieces

From the dark red print, cut:
- 12 E pieces

From the black solid fabric, cut:
- Two 18 × 31-inch pieces

Piecing the Wedding Ring Blocks

1. Referring to **Diagram 1,** sew together a medium green C, a dark green C, a dark red C, and a medium red C piece, as shown. Sew a light red D piece to one end and a light green D reverse piece to the other end, as shown. Press the seam allowances toward one side. Make 32 of these pieced arc units.

Make 32
Diagram 1

2. Referring to **Diagram 2,** sew a black/red print E piece to each end of a pieced arc unit, as shown. Press the seam allowances toward the center of the arc. Make ten of these long pieced arc units.

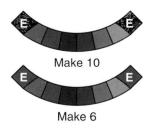

Make 10

Make 6
Diagram 2

3. Referring to **Diagram 2** on page 131, sew a medium red E piece to each end of a pieced arc unit, as shown. Press the seam allowances toward the center of the arc. Make six of these long pieced arc units.

4. Before assembling the wedding rings, check to make sure that ten of the long pieced arc units have black/red print E pieces at each end, that six long pieced arc units have medium red E pieces at each end, and that there are 16 short pieced arc units remaining, with no E pieces at either end.

5. Referring to **Diagram 3,** sew a short pieced arc unit to one side of a focal print B piece, as shown. Press the seam allowance toward the B piece. For more information on sewing curved seams, follow the steps in the tip box for the Cherry Basket quilt on page 59.

6. Referring to **Diagram 3,** sew a long pieced arc unit with medium red E pieces at each end to the other side of the same B piece, as shown. Press the seam allowance toward the B piece. Make six of these pieced arc units.

7. Referring to **Diagram 4,** sew a short pieced arc unit to one side of each remaining B piece, as shown. Sew a long pieced arc unit with dark red E pieces at each end to the other sides of these B pieces, as shown. Press the seam allowances toward the B pieces. Make ten of these pieced arc units.

Make 10

Diagram 4

8. Referring to **Diagram 5** and the quilt photograph on page 130, sew a row of six pieced arc units with medium red prints at each end and five focal print A pieces, as shown. Begin and end these seams ¼ inch in from the D and D reverse

Make 6

Diagram 3

Diagram 5

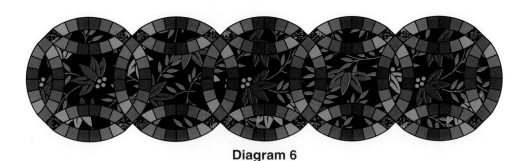

Diagram 6

pieces, as indicated by the dots in the diagram. Press the seam allowances toward the A pieces.

9. Referring to **Diagram 6,** sew the ten pieced arc units with black/red prints on the ends to the remaining sides of the A pieces, as shown.

Assembling the Quilt Top

1. Sew the two pieces of black solid fabric together along the short edges, forming one background piece that measures 18 × 61 inches. Press this seam open.

2. Referring to the **Quilt Diagram,** center the Wedding Ring blocks on the black background fabric and appliqué them by hand or machine, as desired. For information on hand and machine appliqué, see pages 157–159.

3. After the Wedding Rings have been appliquéd, trim the excess background fabric from behind the Wedding Rings to ¼ inch from the appliquéd stitching. This will allow you to quilt through fewer layers of fabric.

Quilting and Finishing

1. Mark quilting designs as desired. The quilt shown is quilted in the ditch round each piece.

2. Layer the quilt top, batting and back; baste. Trim the back and batting to approximately 3 inches larger than the quilt top on all sides.

3. Quilt all marked quilting designs, adding additional quilting as desired.

4. From the binding fabric, make approximately 170 inches of double-fold, straight-grain

binding. For instructions on making and attaching binding, see page 164.

5. Sew the binding to the quilt top. Trim the excess batting and backing. Using thread to match the binding, hand finish the binding with an invisible stitch on the back of the quilt.

Quilt Diagram

Christmas Hunter's Star

Quiltmaker: Gretchen Hudock

Gretchen loves finding a simple approach to complex traditional patterns that even beginners can manage with ease. Piecing an eight-pointed star can often be tricky, but this Hunter's Star is a snap. In this elegant Christmas wall quilt, the spaces between the arrows form eight-pointed stars, symbolizing the night sky over Bethlehem.

Skill Level: Easy

Size: Finished quilt is 44½ inches square
Finished block is 9 inches square

Fabrics and Supplies

- ✓ 1¾ yards of green print fabric for the blocks, borders, and binding
- ✓ 1½ yards of burgundy-with-stars fabric for the blocks and borders
- ✓ 1½ yards of cream print fabric for the blocks and borders
- ✓ 2¾ yards of fabric for the quilt back
- ✓ Crib-size batting (45 × 60 inches)

Cutting

The instructions are for quick cutting the pieces with a rotary cutter and ruler. All measurements include ¼-inch seam allowances. Measurements for the borders are longer than needed; trim them to the exact length when they are added to the quilt top.

From the green print fabric, cut:
- Four 2¼ × 48-inch outer border strips
- Two 7⅛-inch strips across the width of the fabric (approximately 34 inches after the borders are cut). Cut these strips into eight 7⅛-inch squares; cut these squares in half diagonally to make 16 A triangles.
- Two 8-inch strips across the width of the fabric (approximately 34 inches after the borders are cut). Cut these strips into 2½ × 8-inch B strips. You will need a total of 16 B strips.

From the burgundy fabric, cut:
- Four 1¾ × 48-inch middle border strips
- Three 5½-inch strips across the width of the fabric (approximately 35 inches after the borders are cut). Cut these strips into 2½ × 5½-inch C strips. You will need a total of 32 C strips.

From the cream print fabric, cut:
- Four 1½ × 48-inch inner border strips
- Two 7⅛-inch strips across the width of the fabric (approximately 36 inches after the borders are cut). Cut these strips into eight 7⅛-inch squares; cut these squares in half diagonally to make 16 A triangles.
- Two 8-inch strips across the width of the fabric (approximately 36 inches after the borders are cut). Cut these strips into 2½ × 8-inch B strips. You will need a total of 16 B strips
- Three 5½-inch strips across the width of the fabric (approximately 36 inches after the borders are cut). Cut these strips into 2½ × 5½-inch C strips. You will need a total of 32 C strips.

Making the Arrow Bases

1. To make one arrow base, pin a burgundy C strip to each end of a cream B strip with right sides together and the raw edges aligned, as shown in **Diagram 1.** Sew diagonally across the overlapping areas, as shown.

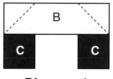

Diagram 1

2. Trim away the excess fabric at the corners of the strip, as shown in **Diagram 2,** leaving ¼-inch seam allowances.

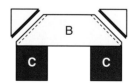

Diagram 2

3. Open the completed arrow base, as shown in **Diagram 3,** and press the seams toward the burgundy fabric.

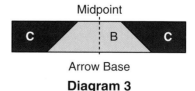

Midpoint

Arrow Base
Diagram 3

4. Repeat to make a total of 16 burgundy and cream arrow bases.

5. In the same manner, sew a cream C strip to each end of the 16 green B strips. Make a total of 16 green and cream arrow bases. Trim the seam allowances to ¼ inch and press them toward the green fabric.

Piecing the Blocks

1. Referring to **Diagram 3** on page 135, fold a burgundy and cream arrow base in half and lightly crease the midpoint.

2. Crease the midpoint on the long side of a cream A triangle, as shown in **Diagram 4.**

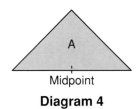

Midpoint

Diagram 4

3. Referring to **Diagram 5,** place right sides together and match the midpoints. Sew the long side of the cream A triangle to the burgundy and cream arrow base, creating the arrow portion of the block. **NOTE:** The arrow base will be longer than the A triangle.

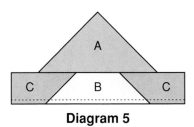

Diagram 5

4. Press the seam toward the arrow base. Using a rotary cutter and ruler, trim the ends of the arrow base to match the A triangle, as shown in **Diagram 6.** Repeat to make a total of 16 cream arrows.

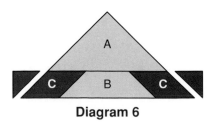

Diagram 6

5. Referring to **Diagram 6,** sew the green A triangles to the green and cream arrow bases to make 16 green arrows.

6. Referring to the **Block Diagram,** complete the Hunter's Star block by sewing a green arrow to a cream arrow. Press the seam toward the green arrow.

Block Diagram

SQUARING UP A BLOCK

A quilt top is easier to assemble if all of the blocks are exactly the same size. Try this trick to make sure your blocks are straight and true: Make a square precisely the size of your block from template plastic and place masking tape on it from corner to corner. Lay this plastic square over each block, lining the diagonal taped line with the block diagonal. If necessary, trim the block to size with a rotary cutter or make light pencil marks and trim away any excess fabric with scissors. ◆

Assembling the Quilt Top

1. Referring to the **Quilt Diagram** for color placement, lay the blocks out in four horizontal rows of four blocks each.

2. Sew the blocks together into rows and press the seams in opposite directions.

3. Sew the rows of blocks together and press the seams between rows in opposite directions.

4. Referring to the **Quilt Diagram,** make a triple border by sewing a 1½-inch cream inner border strip, a burgundy middle border strip, and a green outer border strip together along the long sides. Make four triple borders and mark the midpoint of each border.

5. Mark the midpoint on each side of the quilt top. Referring to the **Quilt Diagram,** match the midpoints of the triple borders to each side of the quilt top. Pin a triple border to each side of the quilt. Sew each border to the quilt top, beginning and ending ¼ inch in from each edge of the quilt and miter the corner seams. For more information on mitered corners, see page 160.

Quilting and Finishing

1. Layer the quilt back, batting, and quilt top; baste. Trim the quilt back and batting so they are approximately 3 inches larger than the quilt top on all sides.

2. Quilt as desired. The quilt shown is machine quilted in the ditch around the pieces in each block and in the ditch of the border seams. Lines are quilted diagonally through the center of each arrow.

3. From the green print fabric, make approximately 190 inches of double-fold binding. For more information on making and attaching binding, see page 164.

4. Sew the binding to the quilt top. Trim the excess batting and backing. With matching thread and a blind stitch, sew the binding to the back of the quilt.

5. Make a hanging sleeve for the quilt. Refer to page 167 for more information on how to construct a hanging sleeve.

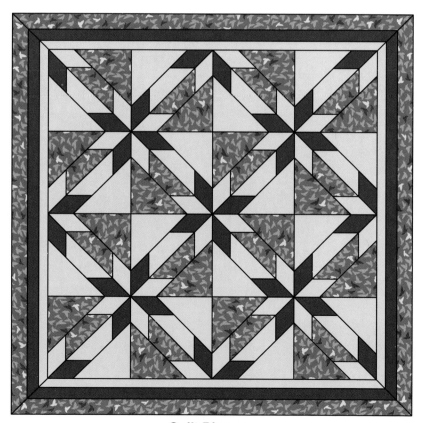

Quilt Diagram

Flower Basket Quilt

Quiltmaker: Cyndi Hershey

Cyndi loves to add an element of surprise to her quilts. The basket on her clever wall quilt is a handy triangular pocket that can be used to hold silk or dried flower arrangements. In red and white prints, this quilt would be a great way to display Valentines or Christmas greenery. The possibilities are endless for varying the color scheme to create a wall quilt suitable for any special occasion or holiday.

Skill Level: Easy

Size: Finished quilt is 30½ × 38½ inches

Fabrics and Supplies

✓ 1 yard of blue floral print fabric for the setting triangles, outer borders, and binding

✓ ⅝ yard of white print fabric for the basket background and pieced borders

✓ ⅜ yard of bright blue print fabric for the basket and pieced borders

✓ ¼ yard *each* of lavender and blue-green print fabric for the inner borders and pieced border squares

✓ ½ yard of very thin batting, such as Thermore or Pellon fleece, for the basket

✓ ½ yard of featherweight nonwoven interfacing for the basket

✓ 1 yard of fabric for the quilt back

✓ Crib-size batting (45 × 60 inches)

Cutting

The instructions are for quick cutting the inner borders, the basket block, setting triangles, and pieced borders with a rotary cutter and ruler. All measurements include ¼-inch seam allowances. Measurements for the borders are slightly longer than needed; trim them to the exact length when adding them to the quilt top.

From the blue floral print fabric, cut:
• Two 11⅜-inch squares. Cut these squares in half diagonally to make 4 D triangles.

• Four 2⅝ × 36-inch strips for the outer borders

• Reserve the remaining fabric for the binding

From the white print fabric, cut:
• One 12½-inch basket background square

• Two 3½ × 9½-inch B rectangles

• One 6⅞-inch-square. Cut this square in half diagonally to make 2 C triangles. Use one for this quilt and set the other aside for a future project.

• Two 3⅞ × 44-inch strips. Cut these strips into sixteen 3⅞-inch squares; cut these squares in half diagonally to make 32 F triangles.

From the bright blue fabric, cut:
• One 12½-inch basket square

• One 3⅞-inch square. Cut this square in half diagonally to make 2 A triangles.

• Six 3½-inch E squares

From the lavender fabric, cut:
• Two 2½ × 28-inch inner border strips

• Four 3½-inch E squares for the pieced borders

From the blue-green fabric, cut:
• Two 2½ × 33-inch inner border strips

• Four 3½-inch E squares

From both the interfacing and the fleece, cut:
• One 12½-inch square

Piecing the Flower Basket Block

1. Place the square of interfacing and the very thin batting on the wrong side of the bright blue 12½-inch basket square. Fold all layers in half diagonally, with wrong sides together. Baste the raw edges together. Using matching thread, machine quilt a 3-inch grid parallel to the short sides of the triangle, as shown in **Diagram 1**. Also quilt across the intersections of the grid, parallel to the long side of the triangle, as shown.

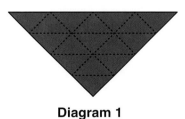

Diagram 1

2. Place the blue basket triangle on top of the white basket background square, as shown in **Diagram 2** on page 140, carefully matching the raw edges, and baste them together along the seam allowances.

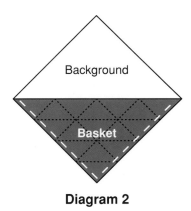

Diagram 2

3. Sew an A triangle to a B rectangle, as shown in **Diagram 3.** Repeat to make another A/B unit, reversing positions, as shown.

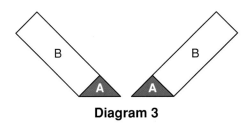

Diagram 3

4. Sew one A/B unit to the lower right side of the basket block, as shown in **Diagram 4.** Press the seams toward the A/B unit. In the same manner, sew the other A/B unit to the lower left side, as shown.

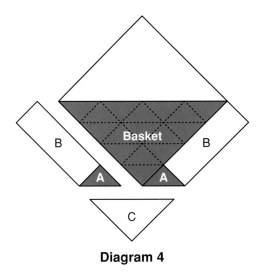

Diagram 4

5. Referring to **Diagram 4,** sew a white C triangle to the basket base, completing the basket block. Press the seam toward the white C triangle.

Assembling the Quilt Top

1. Sew a blue floral print D triangle to each side of the completed basket block and press the seams toward the D triangles.

2. Measure the width of the quilt top. Trim the lavender inner borders to this measurement and sew them to the top and bottom edges of the quilt top. Press the seams toward the borders.

3. Measure the length of the quilt top, including the lavender borders. Trim the blue-green inner border strips to this measurement and sew them to the side edges of the quilt top. Press the seams toward the borders.

4. In the same manner, add the four blue floral print outer borders to the quilt top.

SETTING BLOCKS ON POINT

To help make sure that the D triangles are even on all sides of the basket block, fold each D triangle in half and crease the midpoint on the long side. Then mark the midpoint on each side of the basket block. Pin the center point of one D triangle to one side of the basket block. Sew two D triangles to opposite sides of the basket block, taking care not to stretch the bias edge of the D triangles. Press the seams toward the D triangles. Trim the points that extend beyond the sides of the basket block. In the same manner, pin and sew the two remaining D triangles to the basket block. ◆

Making the Pieced Borders

1. Referring to the photograph on page 138 for color placement, lay out seven E squares on point, with white F triangles between them, as shown in **Diagram 5.**

Diagram 5

2. Sew a white F triangle to two opposites of all of the border squares, as shown in **Diagram 6.** Press the seams toward the E squares.

Diagram 6

3. Sew the borders together, adding a white F triangle to each end, as shown in **Diagram 7.** With a rotary cutter and ruler, trim the triangles at the ends of the borders, as shown, leaving a ¼-inch seam allowance at each end.

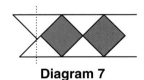

Diagram 7

4. Referring to the **Quilt Diagram,** sew the pieced borders to the top and bottom of the quilt. Press the seams toward the floral print borders.

Quilting and Finishing

1. Layer the quilt back, batting, and quilt top; baste. Trim the quilt back and batting so they are approximately 3 inches larger than the quilt top on all sides.

2. Mark quilting designs as desired. The quilt shown is quilted in the ditch of the patchwork seams. Continue the lines of the grids quilted in the basket base across the top portion of the white background square, taking care to lift the basket out of the way when quilting. Add additional quilting as desired.

3. From the floral print fabric, make approximately 150 inches of double-fold binding. For instructions on making and attaching binding, see page 164.

4. Sew the binding to the quilt top. Trim the excess batting and backing, and hand finish the binding on the back of the quilt. Add a hanging sleeve, following the instructions on page 167.

Quilt Diagram

Hearts and Tulips

Quiltmaker: Cyndi Hershey

What lovelier symbols of spring could there be than hearts and tulips? With plenty of space for delicate quilting, this would be a great gift for your favorite Valentine. Or if the white areas were left unquilted, family members could inscribe special messages to create a beautiful memory quilt for Mother's Day.

Skill Level: Easy

Size: Finished quilt is 36½ inches square
Finished block is 6 inches square

Fabrics and Supplies

- ✓ 1⅞ yards of white-on-white print fabric for the heart blocks, tulip units, and binding
- ✓ ½ yard of pink and teal floral print fabric for the heart blocks
- ✓ ⅝ yard of teal print fabric for the tulip units
- ✓ ¼ yard of light pink print fabric for the tulip units
- ✓ ¼ yard of dark pink print fabric for the tulip units
- ✓ 1¾ yards of fabric for the quilt back
- ✓ Crib-size batting (45 × 60 inches)
- ✓ Rotary cutter, ruler, and mat

Cutting

Instructions are for quick cutting the pieces with a rotary cutter and ruler. All measurements include ¼-inch seam allowances. In some cases, quick cutting may result in leftover pieces.

From the white-on-white print fabric, cut:
- Two 6½-inch × 44-inch strips. Cut these strips into 6½-inch F squares. You will need a total of 8 F squares.
- One 6⅞× 44-inch strip. Cut this strip into four 6⅞-inch squares; cut these squares in half diagonally to make 8 G triangles.
- Three 3⅞ × 44-inch strips. Cut these strips into twenty-four 3⅞-inch squares; cut these squares in half diagonally to make 48 D triangles.
- Three 2⅜ × 44-inch strips. Cut these strips into forty 2⅜-inch squares; cut these squares in half diagonally to make 80 B triangles.
- Two 2 × 44-inch strips. Cut these strips into 2-inch E squares. You will need a total of 24 E squares.

From the pink and teal print fabric, cut:
- One 3⅞ × 44-inch strip. Cut this strip into eight 3⅞-inch squares; cut these squares in half diagonally to make 16 D triangles.
- Two 2 × 44-inch strips. Cut these strips into 2 × 3½-inch C rectangles. You will need a total of 16 C rectangles.
- One 4¼ × 44-inch strip. Cut this strip into four 4¼-inch squares; cut these squares in half diagonally in both directions to make 16 A triangles.

From the teal print fabric, cut:
- Three 3⅞ × 44-inch strips. Cut these strips into twenty-four 3⅞-inch squares; cut these squares in half diagonally to make 48 D triangles.

From the light pink print fabric, cut:
- One 2 × 44-inch strip. Cut this strip into 2-inch E squares. You will need a total of 12 E squares.
- One 2⅜ × 44-inch strip. Cut this strip into twelve 2⅜-inch squares; cut these squares in half diagonally to make 24 B triangles.

From the dark pink print fabric, cut:
- One 2 × 44-inch strip. Cut this strip into 2-inch E squares. You will need a total of 12 E squares.
- One 2⅜ × 44-inch strip. Cut this strip into twelve 2⅜-inch squares; cut these squares in half diagonally to make 24 B triangles.

Piecing the Heart Blocks

1. Referring to **Diagram 1,** sew two white B triangles to a pink and teal A triangle, as shown. Press the seam allowances toward the B triangles. Repeat to make another unit like this.

Diagram 1

2. Referring to **Diagram 2,** sew together two pink and teal C rectangles, as shown. Press this seam allowance to one side. Repeat to make another unit like this.

Diagram 2

3. Referring to **Diagram 3** on page 144, sew a white D triangle to a pink and teal D triangle. Press the seam allowance toward the white D triangle. Repeat to make another unit like this.

Diagram 3

4. Referring to **Diagram 4,** sew the units from Steps 1 through 3 into three horizontal rows, as shown. Press these seam allowances to one side. This completes one heart block.

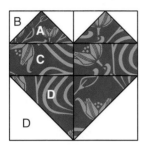

Heart Block
Diagram 4

5. Sew the three horizontal rows together, completing a heart block, as shown. Press these seam allowances toward the bottom of the block.

6. Repeat Steps 1 through 5 to make a total of eight heart blocks.

Piecing the Tulip Units

1. Referring to **Diagram 5,** sew a light pink B triangle to a white B triangle, as shown. Press the seam allowance toward the pink triangle. Repeat to make another triangle-pieced square like this.

Diagram 5

2. Referring to **Diagram 6,** sew a white E square to one of the triangle-pieced squares. Press the seam allowance toward the white E square. Repeat to make another unit, this time using a pink E square, as shown. Press this seam allowance toward the pink E square.

3. Referring to **Diagram 7,** sew the square and triangle-pieced square units together. Press the seam allowance toward the pink E square.

Diagram 6

Diagram 7

4. Referring to **Diagram 8,** sew a teal D triangle to each side of the unit made in Step 3. Press the seam allowances toward the teal D triangles. This completes one tulip unit.

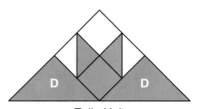

Tulip Unit
Diagram 8

5. Repeat Steps 1 through 4 to make a total of 12 tulip units containing light pink print B triangles and E squares and 12 tulip units containing dark pink print B triangles and E squares.

Assembling the Quilt Top

1. Referring to the **Center Block Diagram,** sew four tulip units to each side of a heart block, as shown. Press the seam allowances toward the heart block. Repeat to make a total of four blocks.

Center Block Diagram

Piecing the Border Units

To complete the quilt top, make the top, bottom, and side border units, referring to the **Quilt Diagram.**

1. Sew together a heart block, a white F square, a white G triangle, and a tulip unit, as shown in **Diagram 9.** Press the seam allowances toward the heart block. Repeat to make another border unit like this.

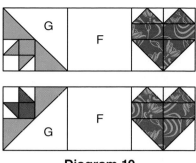

Diagram 10

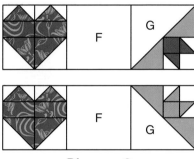

Diagram 9

2. Reversing the piecing order of the previous step, sew together two more border units, as shown in **Diagram 10.**

3. Sew together a top border unit and a bottom border unit, as shown in **Diagram 11.**

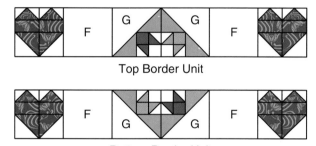

Top Border Unit

Bottom Border Unit

Diagram 11

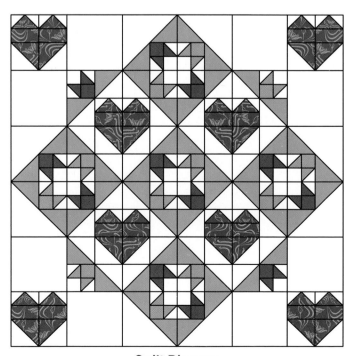

Quilt Diagram

4. To make a border unit for the side of the quilt, sew together an F square, a G triangle, and two tulip units, a G triangle, and an F square, as shown in **Diagram 12.** Repeat to make a second side border unit like this.

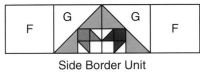

Side Border Unit
Diagram 12

Assembling the Quilt Top

1. Referring to the **Quilt Diagram** on page 145, sew two of the large center blocks together. Press the seam allowance to one side. Repeat for the remaining two large center blocks, pressing the seam allowance in the opposite direction.

2. Sew the four large center blocks together. Press this seam allowance to one side.

3. Sew a side border unit to each side of four center blocks, as shown in the **Quilt Diagram.** Press these seams toward the border units.

4. Sew a top/bottom border unit to the top and bottom edges of the quilt top, as shown. Press these seam allowances toward the border units.

Quilting and Finishing

1. Mark all quilting designs. The quilt shown is quilted in the ditch around each of the heart and tulip shapes. The **Quilting Diagram** shows the quilting for the center heart blocks, white F squares, and white G triangles.

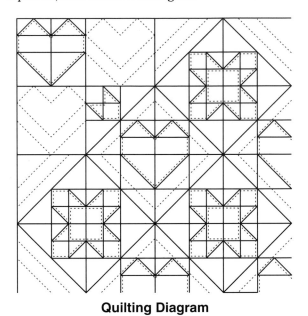

Quilting Diagram

2. Layer the quilt back, batting and quilt top; baste. Trim the quilt back and batting 3 inches larger than the quilt top on all sides.

3. Quilt all marked quilting designs, adding additional quilting as desired.

4. From the binding fabric, make approximately 160 inches of double-fold binding. See page 164 for instructions on making and attaching binding.

5. Sew the binding to the quilt top. Trim the excess batting and backing. Use matching thread and an invisible stitch to hand finish the binding on the back of the quilt.

Thanksgiving Wall Quilt

Quiltmaker: Kathy Berschneider

Kathy searched everywhere to find the perfect fabrics for her autumn wall quilt. After visiting all of the stores near her home in Rockford, Illinois, she finally found the focal print she wanted in Sun Prairie, Wisconsin. With a Thanksgiving theme in mind, she selected warm autumn tones for the Indian Trails blocks, although in different colors, this pattern would also make a nice quilt for other holidays.

Skill Level: Easy

Size: Finished quilt is 31 × 31 inches
Finished block is 6 inches square

Fabrics and Supplies

NOTE: A multicolored focal fabric is an interesting, medium- to large-scale print.

✓ ¾ yard of focal fabric for the blocks
✓ ¼ yard of focal or other fabric for the binding
✓ ⅝ yard of teal print for the blocks
✓ ½ yard of light orange print for the blocks
✓ ½ yard of orange plaid for the blocks
✓ 1 yard of muslin for the quilt back
✓ Crib-size batting (45 × 60 inches)

Cutting

This quilt is quick cut using a rotary cutter and ruler, without templates. All measurements include ¼-inch seam allowances.

From the focal fabric, cut:
• Four 2¼ × 44-inch border strips
• Two 5¾ × 44-inch strips. Cut these strips into eight 5⅜-inch squares; cut these squares in half diagonally to make 16 triangles.

From the orange plaid, cut:
• Two 5¾ × 44-inch strips. Cut these strips into eight 5⅜-inch squares; cut these squares in half diagonally to make 16 triangles.

From the teal print, cut:
• Four 1¾ × 44-inch border strips
• Three 2⅜ × 44-inch strips. Cut these strips into forty-eight 2⅜-inch squares; cut these squares in half diagonally to make 96 triangles.

From the light orange print, cut:
• Three 2⅜ × 44-inch strips. Cut these strips into forty-eight 2⅜-inch squares; cut these squares in half diagonally to make 96 triangles.
• One 2 × 44-inch strip. Cut strip into 2-inch squares. You will need a total of 16 squares; do not cut these squares in half.

Piecing the Blocks

1. Stitch a teal triangle to a light orange triangle, as shown in **Diagram 1.** Press the seams toward the light orange triangle. Make 96 triangle-pieced squares.

2. Sew three teal and light orange triangle-pieced squares together, as shown in **Diagram 2,** forming the green points for one side of the block.

Diagram 1   **Diagram 2**

3. Sew a 2-inch light orange square to one end of this row, as shown in **Diagram 3.** Make 16 of these rows for the right side of the block.

4. Sew together a row of three triangle-pieced squares for the left side of the block, reversing the positions of the colors, as shown in **Diagram 4.**

Diagram 3   **Diagram 4**

5. Sew the large focal print triangles to the plaid triangles, as shown in the **Block Diagram.**

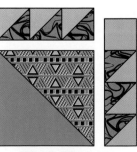

Block Diagram

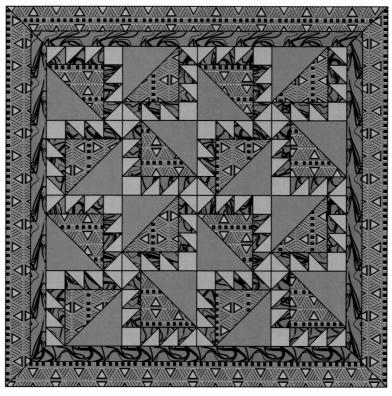

Quilt Diagram

6. Referring to the **Block Diagram,** sew the shorter row of triangle-pieced squares to the side of the large focal print and plaid triangle-pieced square. Press the seams toward the focal print. Sew the longer row of triangle-pieced squares to the other side of the large triangle-pieced square. Make a total of 16 blocks.

Assembling the Quilt Top

Lay the blocks out in four rows of four blocks, as shown in the **Quilt Diagram.** Sew the blocks together into four rows. Press the seams in alternate directions. Sew the rows of blocks together. Press the seams in opposite directions.

Adding the Borders

1. Sew the teal border strips to the focal fabric border strips. The border pieces will be longer than necessary and will be trimmed later.

2. Sew the top and bottom borders to the quilt top, starting and stopping ¼ inch in from the edges of the quilt top. Do not press these seams. Repeat this process with the side borders.

3. Miter the corners of the borders. For instructions on mitering corners, see page 160.

Quilting and Finishing

1. Mark the quilt top for quilting. Kathy elected to quilt in the ditch around individual pieces so no marking was necessary.

2. Layer the quilt back, batting, and quilt top; baste. Trim the quilt back and batting so they are approximately 3 inches larger than the quilt top on all sides. Quilt as desired.

3. From the binding fabric, make approximately 130 inches of double-fold binding. See page 164 for suggested binding widths and instructions on making and attaching binding.

4. Sew the binding to the quilt top. Trim the excess batting and backing, and hand finish the binding on the back of the quilt.

5. To make a sleeve to hang your finished wallhanging, hem the short ends of an 8½ × 31-inch strip of fabric and sew it into a tube. Hand stitch the sleeve to the upper back edge of the quilt. For more instructions on making a hanging sleeve, see page 167.

Tips and Techniques

In this chapter you'll find detailed descriptions of general quiltmaking techniques as well as hints and tips designed to make your qluiltmaking successful and fun.

Supplies to Have on Hand

"Quiltmaking Basics" describes the supplies you'll need to get started on the projects in this book. "Quiltmaking Time-Savers" describes quilting tools that you may want to work with. A few of the projects also require specialized supplies; those supplies are listed with the projects.

Quiltmaking Basics

- **Needles.** Use *sharps* for hand sewing and appliqué and *betweens* for hand quilting. For both sharps and betweens, the larger the number, the smaller the needle. The general rule is to start with the larger-size needles and move to smaller ones as you gain experience. Experiment with different sizes to see which are most comfortable in your hand and the easiest to manipulate through the fabric.

- **Straight pins.** Do not use pins that have become burred or rusted; they may leave marks in your fabric. Long (1½-inch) pins with glass or plastic heads are easy to work with, especially when pinning layers.

- **Scissors.** If you are cutting your fabric with scissors, use a good, sharp pair of dressmaker's shears. Use these only on fabric. You should also have a pair of small, sharp embroidery scissors for trimming threads and seam allowances and a pair of general scissors for cutting paper and template plastic.

- **Iron and ironing board.** Careful pressing is important for accurate piecing. To save steps and increase efficiency, keep your ironing board and iron close to your sewing area.

- **Sewing machine.** Keep it clean, oiled, and in good working order.

- **Template plastic or cardboard.** Templates are rigid master patterns used to mark patchwork and appliqué shapes on fabric. Thin, semitransparent plastic, available in sheets at quilt and craft shops, is ideal, although poster-weight cardboard can also be used for templates.

- **Thread.** Always use good-quality thread. For sewing, use either 100 percent cotton or cotton-covered polyester. For quilting, use special quilting thread.

Quiltmaking Time-Savers

- **Rotary cutter and cutting mat.** For greater speed and accuracy, you can cut all border strips and many other pieces with a rotary cutter instead of scissors. You must always use a specially designed cutting mat when working with a rotary cutter. The self-healing surface of the mat protects the work surface and helps to grip the fabric to keep it from slipping. An all-purpose cutting mat size is 18 × 24 inches. See the section on rotary cutting on page 000 for tips on using the cutter.

- **See-through ruler.** The companion to the rotary cutter and mat is the see-through plastic ruler. It comes in several sizes and shapes; a useful size to have on hand is a 6 × 24-inch heavy-duty ruler that is marked in inches, quarter inches, and eighth inches and has a 45 degree angle line for mitering. Also handy are a ruled plastic square, 12 × 12 inches or larger, and a 6 × 12-inch ruler for cutting segments from strip sets.

- **Plastic-coated freezer paper.** Quilters have discovered many handy uses for this type of paper, which is stocked in grocery stores with other food-wrapping supplies. Choose a quality brand, such as Reynolds.

About Fabric

Since fabric is the most essential element in a quilt, what you buy and how you treat it are important considerations. Buy the best that you can afford; you'll be far happier with the results if you work with good-quality materials. Read through this section for additional tips on selecting and preparing fabric.

Selecting Fabrics

The instructions for each of the quilts in this book include the amount of fabric you will need. When choosing falrics, most experienced quilters insist on 100 percent cotton broadcloth, or dress-weight, fabric. It presses well and handles easily, whether you are sewing by hand or machine.

If there is a quilt specialty shop in your area, the sales staff there can help you choose fabrics. Most home-sewing stores also have a section of all-cotton fabrics for quilters. If you have scraps left over from other sewing, use them only if they are all-cotton and all of similar weight.

CONSTRUCT A DESIGN WALL

There are several different ways to construct a design wall, using foam core board, white flannel, felt, fleece, or cotton batting. If you have the space to accommodate a design surface in your sewing room, start by purchasing a sheet of foam core board at any home improvement store. To cover a design wall that is 38 inches square or smaller, simply cut a length of 45-inch-wide white flannel approximately 3 inches larger than the board on all sides. Stretch the fabric tautly over the board, pulling the excess to the back side. Use thumbtacks or staples to secure the fabric on the back side of the board.

For versatility, a freestanding design wall is great. Just cover two large foam core boards using 72-inch white flannel and hinge them together. That way, it will be easy to fold and tuck the unit into a closet or slide under a bed for storage. ❖

Gaining Color Confidence

Deciding on a color scheme and choosing the fabrics can seem daunting to a beginner. You can take some of the mystery out of the process by learning the basics of color theory. Consult books on color theory, or seek out a class at a local quilt shop or quilt conference. Learn how helpful a color wheel can be, and understand the importance of value (the lightness or darkness of a color) and scale (the size of the print). Your color confidence will grow as you learn the basics and then experiment with different combinations.

Purchasing Fabrics

The yardages given for projects in this book are based on 44- to 45-inch-wide fabrics. These yardages are adequate for both the template and rotary-cutting methods. They have been double-checked for accuracy and always include a little extra. Be aware, however, that fabric is sometimes narrower than the size listed on the bolt, and that any quilter, no matter how experienced, can make a mistake in cutting. It never hurts to buy an extra half-yard of the fabrics for your quilt, just to be safe.

Preparing Fabrics

For best results, prewash, dry, and press your fabrics before using them in your quilts.

Prewashing allows shrinkage to occur and removes finishes and sizing, softening the cloth and making it easier to handle. Washing also allows colors to bleed before light and dark fabrics are combined in a quilt. If one of your fabrics bleeds, set the dye by soaking the whole piece of fabric in a solution of three parts cold water to one part vinegar. Rinse the fabric two or three times in warm water. If the fabric still bleeds, don't use it in your quilt.

FIND THE FADE FACTOR

To check your fabrics for fading, cut a small piece from each new print or solid you buy and tape the pieces to a window that gets lots of sun. After one week, compare the taped snippets of fabric to the original pieces to get a good idea of how quickly those fabrics might fade with continued exposure to sunlight. ❖

Keep in mind that prewashing might remove the lovely finish from chintz and polished cotton. If you want to use these fabrics to add sparkle to your quilts, save them for wallhangings or other items that won't need to be laundered.

To prewash, use your automatic washer, warm water, and a mild detergent. Dry fabric on a medium setting in your dryer or outdoors on a clothesline. It's a good idea to get in the habit of washing all your fabrics as soon as you bring them home, even if you're not planning to use them right away. Then, when you are ready to use a fabric, you won't have to wonder whether it's been washed.

While prewashing is best, some quilters prefer the crispness of unwashed fabric and feel they can achieve more accurate machine-sewn patchwork by using fabric right off the bolt. Some machine quilters like to use unwashed fabric, then wash the project after quilting and binding so the quilt looks crinkled and old-fashioned. The risk in washing after stitching is that colors may bleed.

Cutting the Fabric

For each project in this book, the cutting instructions follow the list of fabrics and supplies. Quilters who prefer the traditional method of making templates and scissor-cutting individual pieces will find full-size patterns or template sizes and cutting guidelines. For quilters who prefer to rotary cut, quick-cutting directions speed things along. You may want to try a combination of techniques, using scissors and templates for certain pattern pieces and the rotary cutter for straight pieces like the borders and bindings.

DUCT TAPE TO THE RESCUE

If you're cutting pieces of fabric that are longer than your cutting mat, consider borrowing a mat from a friend and taping it onto yours. Lay both mats face down and slide the edges together until they meet evenly. Join them together with a strip of duct tape and you'll be ready to turn the mats over and cut long strips of fabric easily. ❖

For some of the projects there are no patterns. Other projects have foundation patterns for paper piecing. In these cases, you will either measure and cut squares, triangles, and rectangles directly from the fabric, or you will be instructed to cut and work with strips of fabric.

Although rotary cutting can be faster and more accurate than cutting with scissors, it

does have one disadvantage: It does not always result in the most efficient use of fabric. In some cases, the quick-cutting method featured in the project will result in long strips of leftover fabric. Don't think of these as wasted bits of fabric; just add these strips to your scrap bag for future projects.

Tips on Rotary Cutting

- Keep the rotary cutter out of children's reach. The blade is extremely sharp!

- Make it a habit to slide the blade guard into place as soon as you stop cutting.

- Always cut *away* from yourself.

- Square off the end of your fabric before measuring and cutting pieces, as shown in **Diagram 1.** Place a ruled square or right-angle triangle on the fold, and place a 6 × 24-inch ruler against the side of the square. Hold the ruler in place, remove the square, and cut along the edge of the ruler. If you are left-handed, work from the other end of the fabric.

6" x 24" ruler

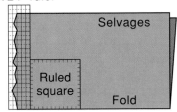

Diagram 1: Square off the uneven edges of the fabric before cutting the strips.

- Use the right cutter for the job. The large size is best for cutting several layers. The small cutter is ideal for cutting around thick plastic

templates since it is easier to control around curves and points.

- When cutting strips or rectangles, cut on the crosswise grain, as shown in **Diagram 2,** unless instructed otherwise. Strips can then be cut into squares, as shown. You can stack two or three folded strips on top of each other so you have four or six layers of fabric, and you will be cutting squares from all the strips at once.

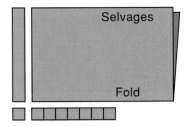

Diagram 2: Cut strips or rectangles on the crosswise grain. Cut the strips into squares.

- Check strips periodically to make sure the fabric is square and the strips are straight, not angled. (See **Diagram 3.**) If your strips are not straight, refold the fabric, making sure the selvages are even, square off the edge, and cut again.

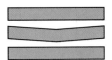

Diagram 3: Check to see that the strips are straight. If they are angled, refold the fabric and square off the edge again.

- Cut triangles from squares, as shown in **Diagram 4.** The project directions will tell you whether to cut the square into two triangles by making one diagonal cut

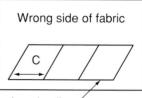

(**Diagram 4A**) or into four triangles by making two diagonal cuts (**4B**).

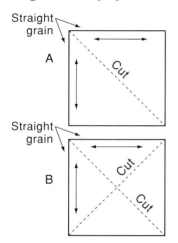

Diagram 4: *Cut two triangles from a square by making one diagonal cut (A). Cut four triangles from a square by making two diagonal cuts (B).*

TAPE YOUR RULERS

Even if the measurement line you need for cutting strips is actually on your rotary cutting ruler, it can be helpful to place a piece of masking tape on the underside of the ruler at whichever line you are using. The edge of the masking tape becomes an important visual guide that keeps you from having to look at all the other lines on the ruler each time you move it across the fabric. ❖

Making and Using Templates

The patterns in this book are printed full size, with no drafting required. For some of the pieced projects, you will have the option of either making templates using the patterns or dimensions given and cutting fabric pieces individually, or using a rotary cutter to quick cut them.

Thin, semitransparent plastic makes excellent, durable templates. Lay the plastic over the book page, carefully trace the patterns onto the plastic, and cut them out with scissors. To make cardboard templates, transfer the patterns to tracing paper, glue the paper to the cardboard, and cut out the templates. Copy identification letters and any grain line instructions onto your templates. Always check your templates against the printed pattern for accuracy.

The patchwork patterns in the book are printed with double lines: an inner dashed line and an outer solid line. If you intend to sew your patchwork by hand, trace the inner dashed line to make finished-size templates. Cut out the templates on the traced line. Draw around the template on the wrong side of the fabric, as shown in **Diagram 5,** leaving ½ inch between lines. The lines you draw are the sewing lines. Then mark the ¼-inch seam allowances before you cut out the fabric pieces.

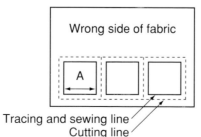

Diagram 5: *If piecing by hand, mark around the template on the wrong side of the fabric. Cut it out, adding ¼-inch seam allowances on all sides.*

If you plan to sew your patchwork by machine, use the outer solid line and make your templates with seam allowances included. Draw around the templates on the wrong side of the fabric, as shown in **Diagram 6.** The line you draw is the cutting line. Sew with an exact ¼-inch seam for perfect patchwork.

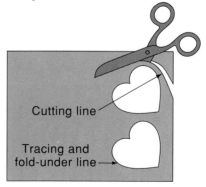

Diagram 6: *If piecing by machine, use templates with seam allowances included.*

Patterns for appliqué pieces are printed with only a single line. Make finished-size templates for appliqué pieces. Draw around templates on the right side of the fabric, as shown in **Diagram 7,** leaving ½ inch between pieces. The lines you draw will be your fold-under lines, or guides for turning under the edges of the appliqué pieces. Then add scant ¼-inch seam allowances as you cut out the pieces.

Diagram 7: *Draw around the templates on the right side of the fabric for appliqué pieces. Add seam allowances as you cut out the pieces.*

HOLD YOUR PENCIL UPRIGHT

When you mark seam lines on fabric for hand piecing, it's a good idea to keep your pencil perpendicular to the marking surface while you mark. Holding it at an angle can move the seam line out of position, which means that your finished work could be inaccurate. ❖

Tips on Piecing

The standard seam allowance for piecing is ¼ inch. For precise patchwork, where the pieces always meet exactly where they should, you must be vigilant about accurate seam allowances. Some sewing machines come with a handy seam allowance guide marked alongside the feed dogs. On other machines, the distance from the needle to the outside of the presser foot is ¼ inch. (Measure your machine to be sure this is accurate.) On machines that have no built-in guides, you can create your own. Measure ¼-inch from the needle and lay down a 2-inch-long piece of masking tape. Continue to add layers of masking tape on top of the first one until you have a raised edge against which you can guide fabric, automatically measuring the ¼-inch seam allowance.

When assembling pieced blocks, keep in mind these basic rules: Combine smaller pieces to make larger units, join larger units into rows or sections, and join sections to complete the blocks. If you follow these rules, you should be able to build most blocks using only straight seams. Setting in pieces at an angle should only be done when necessary. (Pointers appear on the opposite page.)

Lay out the pieces for the block with right sides up, as shown in the project diagram, before you sew. For quilts with multiple blocks, cut out and piece a sample block first to make sure your fabrics work well together and you have cut out the pieces accurately.

Hand Piecing

For hand piecing, use finished-size templates to cut your fabric pieces. Join the pieces by matching marked sewing lines and securing them with pins. Sew with a running stitch from seam line to seam line, as shown in **Diagram 8,** rather than from raw edge to raw edge. As you sew, check to see that your stitching is staying on the lines, and make a backstitch every four or five stitches to reinforce and strengthen the seam. Secure the corners with an extra backstitch.

Diagram 8: *Join the pieces with a running stitch, backstitching every four or five stitches.*

When you cross a seam allowance of previously joined smaller units, leave the seam allowance free rather than stitching it down. Make a backstitch just before you cross, slip the needle through the seam allowance, make a backstitch after you cross, then resume stitching the seam. (See **Diagram 9.**) When your block is finished, press the seam allowances toward the darker fabrics.

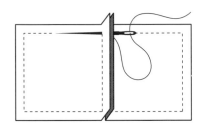

Diagram 9: *When hand piecing, leave the seam allowances free by slipping through without stitching them down.*

THREAD CATCHER

A 3- or 4-inch piece of masking tape makes a great catchall for threads and bits of scrap fabrics. Just make a loop of tape with the sticky side facing outward and place it near your sewing machine. When it's covered with threads and snippets of fabric, stray pins, and needles, or when you're finished working for the day, just toss the tape away. ❖

Machine Piecing

For machine piecing, cut the fabric pieces using templates with seam allowances included or use a rotary cutter to quick cut. Before sewing a block, sew a test seam to make sure you are taking accurate ¼-inch seams. Even $\frac{1}{16}$ inch of inaccuracy can result in a block that is not the right size. Adjust your machine to sew 10 to 12 stitches per inch. Select a neutral-color thread such as a medium gray that blends well with the fabrics you are using.

Join the pieces by sewing from raw edge to raw edge. Press the seams before crossing them with other seams. Since the seam allowances will be stitched down when crossed with another seam, you'll need to think about the direction in which you want them to lie. Press the seam allowances toward darker fabrics whenever possible to prevent them from shadowing through lighter ones. For more information on pressing, see page 156.

GRADE SEAM ALLOWANCES

While it is usually recommended that seam allowances be pressed toward the darker fabric, sometimes the piecing order dictates pressing toward the lighter fabric instead. This can cause the edges of the darker seam allowance to "shadow through." If this happens, simply trim the darker seam allowance to a scant ¼ (or ³⁄₁₆) inch. At a full ¼ inch, the lighter seam allowance will then cover the raw edges of the darker fabric. ❖

When you join blocks into rows, press all the seam allowances in opposite directions from row to row. Then, when you join the rows, abut the pressed seam allowances to produce precise intersections.

In many quilts, you need to sew a large number of the same size or shape pieces together to create units for the blocks. For a bed-size quilt, this can mean a hundred or more squares, triangles, or rectangles that need to be stitched together. A time-saving method known as assembly-line piecing can reduce the drudgery. Run pairs of pieces or units through the sewing machine one after another without cutting the thread, as shown in **Diagram 10.** Once all the units you need have been sewn, snip them apart and press. You can continue to add on more pieces to these units, assembly-line fashion, until the sections are the size you need.

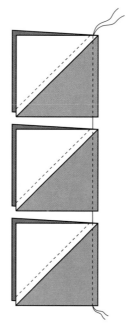

Diagram 10: Feed the units through the machine without cutting the thread.

Setting In Pieces

Not all patchwork patterns can be assembled with continuous straight seams. An example is the August quilt on page 2. Background pieces must be set into the angled openings created by the diamonds. Setting in calls for precise

stitching as you insert pieces into angles, as shown in **Diagram 11.** In this example, pieces A, B, and C are set in to the angles created by the four joined diamond pieces.

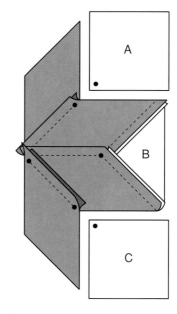

Diagram 11: Setting-in calls for careful matching of points and precise stitching. Here, pieces A, B, and C are set into the angles created by the four joined diamonds.

Setting In by Hand

Setting in by hand is simple. Follow the directions on page 153 to make finished-size templates. Trace the templates, then mark ¼-inch seam allowances before cutting out pieces.

1. Pin the piece to be set in to one side of the angle, right sides together, match corners exactly.

2. Starting ¼ inch from the outside edge and working to the corner, stitch along the marked seam line, as shown in **Diagram 12** on page 156, removing pins as you go. Stop ¼ inch from the inside corner, at your marked seam line. Knot the thread and clip it.

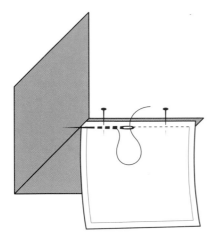

Diagram 12: Pin the pieces right sides together and stitch from the outside into the corner.

3. Bring the adjacent edge up and pin it to the other side of the angle, as shown in **Diagram 13.** Hand stitch the seam from the corner out, stopping ¼ inch from the edge at the end of the marked seam line.

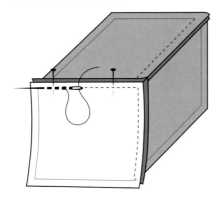

Diagram 13: Pin the adjacent edge to the other side of the angle and stitch from the corner to the outside.

Setting In by Machine

If you are setting in pieces by machine, make special templates that will allow you to mark dots on the fabric at the points where pieces will come together. By matching dots on the pattern pieces as they meet at the angle, you can be sure of a smooth fit. To make these templates, first mark the sewing lines, then use a large needle to pierce a hole at each setting in point. (See **Diagram 14.**) As you trace the templates onto the wrong side of the fabric, push the tip of the pencil through each of these holes to create a dot. Mark all corners of each pattern piece. You may discover later that you want to turn the piece to adjust color or pattern placement; marking all the corners allows you that option.

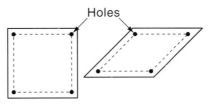

Holes

Diagram 14: For setting-in pieces by machine, make templates with holes at the setting-in points.

1. Pin a piece to one side of the angle with right sides together, matching the dots. Beginning and ending the seam with a backstitch, sew from the raw edge into the corner, and stop the stitching exactly on the marked corner dot. Don't allow any stitching to extend into the seam allowance. (See **Diagram 15.**)

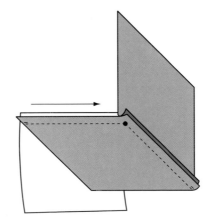

Diagram 15: Pin the piece to one side of the angle, matching dots. Stitch from the edge into the corner.

2. Remove the work from your machine to realign the pieces for the other side of the seam. Swing the other side of the angled piece up, match dots, and pin the pieces together.

3. Sew from the corner dot to the outside edge to complete the seam, again backstitching at the beginning and end. (See **Diagram 16.**) Press the seams toward the set-in piece.

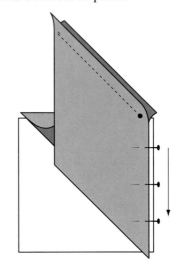

Diagram 16: Matching dots, pin the piece to the other side of the angle. Stitch from the corner dot to the outside edge.

Pressing Basics

Proper pressing can make a big difference in the appearance of a finished block or quilt top. Quilters are divided on the issue of whether a steam or dry iron is best. Experiment to see which works best for you. For each project, pressing instructions are given as needed in the step-by-step directions. Review the list of guidelines that follow to brush up on your general pressing techniques.

- Press a seam before crossing it with another seam.

- Press seam allowances to one side, not open.

- Press seams of adjacent rows of blocks, or rows within blocks, in opposite directions so the pressed seams will abut as the rows are joined. (See **Diagram 17.**)

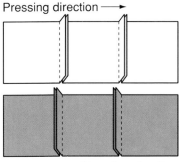

Pressing direction ⟶

⟵ Pressing direction

Diagram 17: Press the seams of adjacent rows in opposite directions. When the rows are placed right sides together to be joined, the pressed seams will abut.

LEATHER FINGERS

When you're pressing seams directionally, try wearing a leather thimble on the index finger of your left hand. The leather will protect your finger while you work with the placement of seam allowances and keep you from being burned by the iron. ❖

- If possible, press seams toward darker fabrics to avoid show-through on the front of the quilt.

- Press, don't iron. Bring the iron down gently and firmly on the fabric from above, rather than rub the iron over the patchwork.

- Avoid pressing appliqués on the right side after they have been stitched to the background fabric. They are prettiest when slightly puffed, rather than flat. To press appliqués, turn the piece over and press gently on the back of the background fabric.

Hand Appliqué

Several of the quilts in this book include beautiful appliqué. The true tests of fine appliqué work are smoothly turned, crisp edges and sharp points; no unsightly bumps or gaps; and nearly invisible stitches.

Depending on your personal preference, there are three popular techniques that can help you achieve flawless appliqué. Each of these methods is described in detail below.

For any of these methods, use thread that matches the appliqué pieces, and stitch the appliqués to the background fabric with a blind hem or appliqué stitch, as shown in **Diagram 18.** Invest in a package of long, thin size 11 or 12 needles marked sharps. Make stitches ⅛ inch apart or closer, and keep them snug.

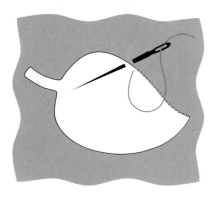

Diagram 18: Stitch the appliqués to the background with a blind hem stitch. The stitches should be nearly invisible.

When constructhg appliqué blocks, always work from background to foreground. When an appliqué piece will be covered or overlapped by another, stitch the underneath piece to the background fabric first.

Basting-Back Method

1. Make finished-size cardboard or thin plastic templates. Mark around the templates on the right side of the fabric to draw fold-under lines. Draw lightly so the lines are thin.

2. Cut out the pieces a scant ¼ inch to the outside of the marked lines.

3. For each appliqué piece, turn the seam allowance under, folding along the marked line, and baste close to the fold with white or natural thread. Clip concave curves and clefts before basting. (See **Diagram 19.**) Do not baste back edges that will be covered by another appliqué.

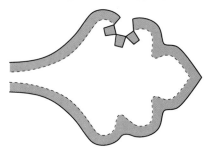

Diagram 19: Clip any concave curves, then baste back the seam allowances.

4. Pin the appliqués in place and stitch them to the background fabric. Remove the basting after the pieces are stitched down.

Freezer Paper Method

1. Make finished-size plastic templates for appliqué patterns.

2. Place templates on the smooth (not shiny) side of the freezer paper and draw around them. Do not add seam allowances. Cut out the patterns along the lines. Make a separate pattern for each appliqué piece.

3. Using a dry iron set on wool, press the paper patterns to the proper fabric, placing the shiny side of the paper on the right side of the fabric. Leave about ½ inch between pieces for seam allowances.

4. Cut out the appliqués ⅛ inch to the outside of the paper edge to allow for seams. Leave the paper attached to the fabric.

5. Pin the appliqué in place on the background fabric with the paper still attached. As you stitch the appliqué to the background, turn under the seam allowance along the edge of the freezer paper, aligning the fold of the fabric with the paper edge. Once the piece is stitched down completely, gently peel off the paper pattern.

Needle-Turn Method

1. Use plastic or cardboard templates to mark finished-size pieces. Mark lightly on the right side of the fabric.

2. Cut out the pieces a generous ⅛ inch larger than the finished size.

3. Pin the pieces in position on the background fabric. Use the tip and shank of your appliqué needle to turn under ½-inch-long sections of seam allowance at a time. As you turn under a section, press it flat with your thumb and then stitch it in place.

Making Bias Strips for Stems and Vines

Fabric strips cut on the bias have more give and are easier to manipulate than strips cut on the straight grain. This makes them ideal for creating beautiful curving stems and vines and twisting ribbons. Bias strips enhance several of the projects in this book, including the Twist and Shout quilt on page 35. The quilt instructions include directions for cutting bias strips the proper width.

Cut bias strips with your rotary cutter using the 45 degree angle line on your see-through ruler. Straighten the left edge of your fabric as described on page 152. Align the 45 degree angle line on your see-through ruler with the bottom edge of the fabric, as shown in **Diagram 20A,** and cut along the edge of the ruler to trim off the corner. Move the ruler across the fabric, cutting parallel strips in the needed width, as shown in **20B.** Once the strips are cut, prepare them for appliqué by using a bias bar as described below.

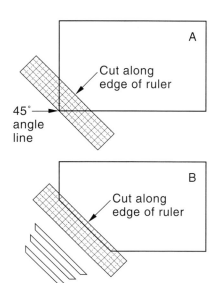

Diagram 20: *Use the 45 degree angle line on your see-through ruler to trim off the corner of the fabric (A). Then move the ruler across the fabric, cutting parallel strips of the width needed (B).*

Narrow bias strips for appliqué can be made using metal or plastic bars called bias bars or Celtic bars. You'll need this type of tool for making the Stars, Leaves, and Currants quilt on page 122, Twist and Shout on page 35, and August on page 2. Bias bars are available in quilt shops and through mail-order catalogs. The bar should be equal to the required finished width of the bias strip.

Cut a fabric strip wide enough to wrap around the bar and to allow for the ⅛-inch seam allowances. Fold the strip in half lengthwise, wrong sides facing, and using a ⅛-inch seam allowance, sew the long raw edges of the strip together. Insert the bar into the tube. Center the seam along the bar and press, as shown in **Diagram 21.** Continue to slide the bar along the tube, pressing as you go. Remove the bar and press the strip one more time.

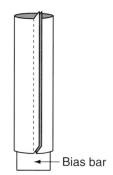

Diagram 21: *Slip bias bar into fabric tube. Center seam along top of bar and press.*

Machine Appliqué

Machine appliqué is ideal for decorative effects. It's a quick-and-easy way to add appliqué pieces to projects that you don't want to spend time hand stitching. Plus, machine appliqué stands up well to repeated washings, so it's great for place mats and clothing.

Satin stitch machine appliqué can be done on any sewing machine that has a zigzag stitch setting. Use a zigzag presser foot with a channel on the bottom that will allow the heavy ridge of stitching to feed evenly. Match your thread to the appliqué pieces. Set your machine for a medium-width zigzag stitch and a very short stitch length. Test stitch on a scrap of fabric. The stitches should form a band of color and be $\frac{1}{8}$ to $\frac{3}{16}$ inch wide. If necessary, loosen the top tension slightly so that the top thread is barely pulled to the wrong side.

1. To prepare the appliqué pieces, use Wonder-Under or a similar paper-backed fusible webbing, following the manufacturer's instructions. For most products, the procedure is the same: Trace the appliqué shapes onto the paper side of the webbing and roughly cut out the the designs, as shown in **Diagram 22.**

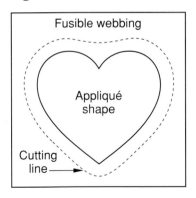

Diagram 22: *Trace the appliqué shape onto the paper side of the webbing and roughly cut out the design.*

2. Using a dry iron set on Wool, fuse the webbing onto the wrong side of the fabrics you have chosen for appliqués.

Cut out the pieces along the tracing lines, as shown in **Diagram 23,** allowing approximately $\frac{1}{4}$-inch underlap on adjacent pieces within a design. Peel off the paper backing, position the pieces on the background fabric, and fuse in place.

Diagram 23: *Fuse the webbing onto the wrong side of the fabric and cut along the tracing line.*

3. Stabilize the background fabric by pinning a sheet of typing paper or commercial stabilizer such as Tear-Away to the wrong side of the background fabric in the areas where you will be stitching. Some quilters like to use freezer paper as a stabilizer for machine appliqué.

4. Machine satin stitch around the edges of the appliqué pieces, covering the raw edges. Change thread colors to match the pieces. When stitching is complete, carefully tear away the stabilizer from the wrong side.

Assembling Quilt Tops

To assemble a quilt comprised of rows of blocks, such as Escargot in Plaid (page 97), refer to the quilt diagram or photograph and lay out all the

pieced or appliqué blocks, plain blocks, and setting pieces right side up, positioned as they will be in the finished quilt.

Pin and sew all the blocks together in vertical or horizontal rows for straight-set quilts and in diagonal rows for diagonal-set quilts. Press the seams in opposite directions from row to row. Join the rows, abutting the pressed seam allowances so the intersections will be accurate.

To keep a large quilt top manageable, join rows into pairs first and then join the pairs, rather than add each row to an increasingly unwieldy top.

When pressing a completed top, press on the back first. Carefully clip and remove hanging threads, then press the front; be sure all the seams are flat.

PHOTOS POINT THE WAY

When deciding on a setting for a sampler quilt, start by laying out the blocks on a floor. That allows you to walk around the blocks and anaylze the balance of color in your arrangement from every angle and then decide how to balance the different types of blocks. Combine the blocks in several different ways, and take an instant film snapshot of each arrangement so you can compare them later and decide on a setting. ❖

Tips for Successful Borders

For most of the quilts in this book, directions for adding the appropriate borders are included with the instructions for that quilt. Here are some general tips that can help you with any quilt you make.

- Cut borders to the desired finished width plus ½ inch for seam allowances. Always cut border strips several inches longer than needed, just to be safe. (Cutting instructions for borders in this book already include seam allowances and extra length.)

- Before adding borders, measure your completed inner quilt top. Measure through the center of the quilt rather than along the edges, which may have stretched from handling. Use this measurement to determine the exact length of your borders. This is an important step; if you don't measure first and simply give the edge of the quilt as much border as it "wants," you may end up with rippled edges on your quilt. Measuring and marking your borders first will allow you to make any necessary adjustment or ease in any fabric that may have stretched along the edge.

- Measure and mark sewing dimensions on the ends of borders before sewing them on, and wait to trim off excess fabric until after sewing.

- Fold border strips in half crosswise and press lightly or mark with a pin to indicate the halfway mark. Align this mark with the center point along the quilt side when pinning on the border.

- Press border seam allowances away from the center of the quilt.

Mitered Borders

Mitered borders add a professional touch to your quilt and are not hard to master if you keep in mind a few basics.

1. Start by measuring your finished quilt top through the center to determine the length the borders should be.

2. If you have multiple borders that are to be mitered, find and mark the center of each border strip. Match the centers, sew the strips together, and treat them as one unit.

3. With a ruler and pencil, mark a ¼-inch sewing line along one long edge of the border strip. For a multiple border, mark the inner strip that goes next to the quilt. Fold the strip in half crosswise and press lightly to mark the halfway point.

4. Starting at the halfway point, measure out in each direction to one-half of the desired finished border length, and make a mark on the sewing line.

5. Use a ruler that has a 45 degree angle line to mark the miter sewing line. Referring to **Diagram 24,** draw a line from the end mark made in Step 4 to the outer edge of the border strip. Mark a cutting line ¼ inch to the outside of the sewing line, but don't trim until after the border is sewn to the quilt top.

6. Pin the marked border strip to the quilt top, matching the crease at the halfway point to the center side of the quilt. Position the end marks on the border strip ¼ inch in from the raw edges of the quilt top. Pin the border to the quilt top, distributing any fullness evenly along the length of the border. Repeat for all remaining border strips.

7. Stitch the borders to the quilt top, starting and stopping at the end marks exactly ¼ inch from each end. Backstitch to secure the stitching. Press the seam allowances away from the quilt top.

8. Sew the miters by folding the quilt diagonally, right sides together, and aligning the marked miter lines on adjacent borders. Stitch from the inner corner mark all the way to the outer raw edge.

9. Check the accuracy of your miter, then trim the excess seam allowance.

Quilting Designs

Exquisite quilting is often the element that makes a quilt truly special. Even a simple quilt can be set apart by the fine workmanship demonstrated by small, even stitches. While some quilts lend themselves to

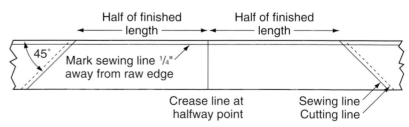

Diagram 24: Mark the border strips for mitering before sewing them to the quilt top.

very simple quilting patterns, such as outline quilting, others are beautifully accented by cables, feathers, and floral designs. Suggestions for quilting designs are included with many of the project instructions. You can duplicate the design the quiltmaker used, create your own, or choose one of the many quilting templates available at quilt shops and through mail-order catalogs.

Some quilting needs no design template. Outline quilting simply follows them seams of the patchwork. It can be in the ditch, that is, right next to the seam, or ¼ inch away from the seam. In-the-ditch quilting needs no marking. For ¼-inch outline quilting, you can work by eye or use ¼-inch-wide masking tape as a guide for stitching. These and other straight lines can also be marked ligltly with a pencil and ruler.

Another type of quilting that needs no marking is called echo quilting. Look at the photo of August (page 2) for a beautiful example of this type of quilting. It contains lines of quilting that outline the sunflowers in concentric rings or shapes. The lines are generally spaced about ½ inch apart.

In contrast to outline and echo quilting, which need no marking, quilting designs, such as the designs for borders in the Stars, Leaves, and Currants quilt (page 122), should be marked before the quilt top is layered with batting and backing. How you mark depends on whether your fabric is light or dark.

Marking Light Fabrics

If your fabric is a light color that you can see through, such

as muslin, you can place the pattern under the quilt top and easily trace the quilting design onto the fabric. First, either trace the design out of the book onto good-quality tracing paper or photocopy it. If necessary, darken the lines with a black permanent marker. If the pattern will be used many times, glue it to cardboard to make it sturdy. Place the pattern under the quilt top and carefully mark the designs on the fabric, making a thin, continuous line that will be covered by the quilting thread. Use a silver quilter's pencil or a mechanical pencil with thin (0.5 mm) medium (B) lead.

Marking Dark Fabrics

Use a white or silver pencil to mark quilting designs on dark fabrics. Mark from the top by drawing around a hard-edged quilting design template. To make simple templates, trace the design onto template plastic and cut out around the outer edge. Then trace around the outer edge of the template onto the fabric, and add inner lines by eye.

You may be able to use the method described above (placing the pattern underneath the fabric) if you place the pattern and the fabric on a light box while marking. The light shining through the paper and fabric will allow you to see the pattern outline through even the darkest fabrics. Any glass-topped table makes an excellent light box area. Simply take the lamp shade off of a small lamp, then place the lamp under the table. Tape your pattern to the tabletop, place the fabric on top of the pattern, and trace the pattern onto the fabric.

Quilt Backings

For each of the projects in this book, the list of fabrics and supplies includes yardage for the quilt back. For wallhangings that are narrower than 44 inches, simply use a full width of yardage cut several inches longer than the quilt top. For the wider wallhangings and most of the bed quilts, the quilt backing must be pieced unless you purchase extra-wide fabric, such as 90- or 108-inch-wide muslin.

Whenever possible, piece quilt backings in two or three panels with the seams running parallel to the long side of the quilt. Backs for quilts such as Hexagons (page 74), which is narrower than 80 inches wide, can easily be pieced this way out of two lengths of yardage. Divide the yardage in half crosswise. Then, to avoid having a seam down the center of the quilt back, divide one of the pieces in half lengthwise. Sew a narrow panel to each side of a full-width central panel, as shown in **Diagram 25.** Be sure to trim the selvages from the yardage before joining the panels. Press the seams away from the center of the quilt.

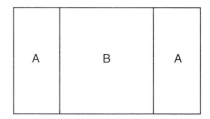

Diagram 25: *Divide the yardage in half crosswise; divide one of the pieces in half lengthwise. Sew one of those halves to each side of the full-width piece, as shown.*

For some quilts, you may make more sensible use of your yardage by piecing the back so that the seams run parallel to the short side of the quilt, as shown in **Diagram 26.** For example, Cherry Basket (page 57) is 87 × 92 inches. To have the seams run parallel to the long side of the quilt, you would need three 3½-yard-long panels, for a total of 10½ yards of fabric. However, if the seams run parallel to the short side of the quilt, you would need three panels, each approximately 2⅝ yards long, for a total of 7⅞ yards of fabric.

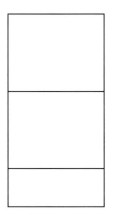

Diagram 26: Divide the yardage crosswise into three equal panels. Sew the three full-width panels together side by side. Layer the backing, batting, and quilt top with the seams running parallel to the short side of the quilt top. Trim the excess from one panel as needed.

To prepare the backing, divide the yardage crosswise into three panels. Trim the selvages and sew the full-width panels together along their long sides. The finished quilt backing should look like the one shown in **Diagram 26.**

Types of Quilt Batting

Quilters generally spend a lot of time selecting the fabrics for their quilts, but often not enough time choosing the batting they will use. When purchasing batting for your quilt, take time to read the manufacturer's literature and think about the intended use of your quilt. Also, talk to experienced quilters about their favorite batting. Experiment with different battings to find which type works best for you. No matter what kind you use, before layering the batting with the quilt backing and top, unfold it and allow it to relax for several hours, or tumble it in the clothes dryer for a few minutes with no heat to remove sharp folds.

Polyester

One hundred percent polyester batting, though lightweight, is very durable and warm. It launders without shrinking and needles easily for hand quilting. One disadvantage of polyester batting is the bearding that often occurs: The fibers migrate through the fabric of the quilt top, creating a fuzzy look. Many polyester battings are bonded, or coated, to reduce bearding. Unfortunately, the bonding makes the batting a little more difficult to needle. Polyester batting comes in many different lofts, which makes it suitable for everything from quilted clothing and home accessories to puffy, tied comforters.

All Cotton

All-cotton battings are popular with quilters who like a very flat, old-fashioned appearance, though some hand quilters think cotton is harder to needle. Unlike polyester, cotton fibers do not beard. At one time, all-cotton batting had to be quilted at very close intervals (¼ to ½ inch) to prevent lumping and migration of the fibers during washing. Some modern cotton battings can be laundered even when quilting is several inches apart. Note that cotton battings will shrink when washed. This is desirable for some quilters who want to create an antique look; the shrinking batting wrinkles the fabrics around the lines of quilting, instantly creating the look of an old quilt.

Cotton/Polyester Blends

Another option is the cotton/polyester blend batting that combines the low-loft sculpted look of cotton with the durability of polyester. This type of batting is easier to needle than the cotton and can be quilted at greater intervals. The fibers are bonded, or coated, to reduce bearding. Some quilters prefer to presoak this type of batting to break down the coating and make the needling easier. Follow the manufacturer's recommendations for pretreating.

Other Options

Keep in mind, too, that batting is not the only option. Cotton flannel gives quilts a flat look that can be ideal for miniature quilts that would be overpowered by puffy batting. Flannel may also be appropriate for items such as tablecloths and table runners, where you don't want a lot of puffiness. Quiltmakers have also used wool and silk battings.

Layering and Basting

Once your quilt top is complete and marked for quilting, your backing is prepared, and your batting is purchased, you are ready to assemble and baste together the layers. Whether you plan to hand or machine quilt, the layers must be assembled securely so that the finished quilt will lie flat and smooth.

Follow the procedure here for successful layering. If you plan to quilt by hand, baste with thread. If you will be machine quilting, use safety pins. Thread basting does not hold the layers securely enough during the machine quilting process. The thread is also more difficult to remove when quilting is completed.

For best results when thread basting large quilts, work at two or three banquet-type tables at a community center, library, or church basement. For pin basting, the best area is a large, clear area on the living room floor with carpet you can pin through when spreading out the quilt back. Whatever surface you work on, make sure it is completely free of dust and dirt before laying the quilt back on it.

Layering

1. Fold the quilt back in half lengthwise and press to form a centerline. Place the back, wrong side up, on the basting table. Position the pressed centerline at the middle of the table. To keep the backing taut, use pieces of masking tape at the corners or clamp it to the table with large binder clips from a stationery store.

2. Fold the batting in half lengthwise and lay it on the quilt backing, aligning the fold with the pressed centerline. Open out the batting; smooth and pat down any wrinkles.

3. Fold the quilt top in half lengthwise, right sides together, and lay it on the batting,

aligning the fold with the center of the batting. Unfold the top; smooth it out and remove any loose threads. Make sure the backing and batting are at least 2 inches larger than the quilt top on all four sides for smaller projects. For bed-size quilts, add 3 inches extra on each side.

Basting

For hand quilting, use a long darning needle and white sewing thread to baste the layers together, making lines of basting approximately 4 inches apart. Baste from the center out in a radiating pattern, or make horizontal and vertical lines of basting in a lattice fashion, using the seams that join the blocks as guidelines.

For machine quilting, use 1-inch safety pins to secure the layers together, pinning from the ceuter out approximately every 3 inches. Be careful not to place the pins where you intend to quilt. You may need as many as 1,000 pins to pin baste a queen-size quilt.

Quilting

Most of the projects in this book are hand quilted, but a few are machine quilted. Whether you will be stitching by hand or by machine, the tips that follow can help with your quilting.

Hand Quilting

- Use a hoop or frame to hold the quilt layers taut and smooth during quilting.

- Use short quilting needles, called betweens, in either size 9 or 10.

- Use quilting thread rather than regular sewing thread. Start with a length of

quilting thread about 18 inches long. This is long enough to keep you going for a while, but not so long that it tangles easily.

- Pop the knot through the fabric at the beginning and end of each length of thread so that no knots show on the quilt front or back. To do this, insert the needle through the top and batting about 1 inch away from where you will begin stitching. Bring the needle to the surface in position to make the first stitch. Gently tug on the thread to pop the knot through the top and bury it in the batting, as shown in **Diagram 27.**

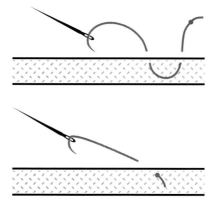

Diagram 27: Insert the needle through the top and batting, and gently tug on the thread until the knot pops through the fabric.

- Quilt by making running stitches, about $\frac{1}{16}$ to $\frac{1}{8}$ inch long, through all three layers. Try to keep the stitches straight and even.

- Thread several needles with quilting thread before you begin, and keep them handy while you work. This way you won't have to stop and thread a needle every time you finish a length of thread.

Machine Quilting

- Use a walking foot (also called an even feed foot) on your sewing machine for quilting straight lines. Use a darning or machine embroidery foot for free-motion quilting.

- To secure the thread at the beginning and end of a design, take several short stitches.

- *For free-motion quilting:* Disengage the sewing machine feed dogs so you can manipulate the quilt freely as you quilt. (Check your sewing machine manual to see how to do this.)

- Choose continuous-line quilting designs so you won't have to begin and end threads as frequently as with interrupted designs.

- Guide the marked design under the needle with both hands, working at an even pace so stitches will be of a consistent length.

Making and Attaching Binding

The most common edge finish for quilts is binding, cut either on the bias or on the straight of grain. Bias binding has more give, which makes it ideal for quilts that have curves or points along the outside edges. Use the yardage reserved for binding to make the type of binding you prefer. Some projects in this book have special edge finishes. Directions for those finishes are included with the quilt projects.

Double-fold binding, also called double-fold binding, is recommended for bed quilts. The bias or straight-grain binding strip is folded in half, and the raw edges are stitched to the edge of the quilt on the right side. The folded edge is then brought to the back of the quilt, as shown in **Diagram 28,** and hand stitched in place. double-fold binding is easier to apply than single-fold binding, and its double thickness adds durability. The strips for this type of binding are cut four times the finished width plus seam allowances. As a general rule, cut the strips 2 inches wide for quilts with thin batting such as cotton and 2¼ inches wide for quilts with thicker batting. Most of the project directions in this book specify double-fold binding, and the fabric yardages are based on that type of binding.

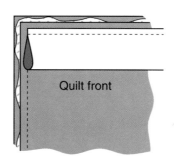

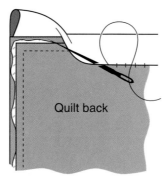

Diagram 28: For double-fold binding, fold the strip in half and stitch it to the quilt front. Bring the folded edge to the back of the quilt and hand stitch it in place.

If you wish to make single-fold binding, cut your fabric strips twice the width of your finished binding plus ½ inch for seam allowances. Press under ¼ inch on one long edge of the binding. This edge will be hand sewn to the back of the quilt. Stitch the other long edge of the binding to the quilt top, right sides together. Fold the binding to the quilt back and stitch in place.

The amount of binding needed for each project is included with the finishing instructions. Generally, you will need the perimeter of the quilt plus 10 to 12 inches for mitering corners and ending the binding. Three-quarters to 1 yard of fabric will usually make enough binding to finish a large quilt.

Follow the instructions here to make continuous-cut bias binding or to join straight strips for continuous straight-grain binding. Unless the project directions tell you otherwise, sew the binding to the quilt as described below, mitering the binding at the corners.

Continuous-Cut Bias Binding

Continuous-cut bias binding is cut in one long strip from a square of fabric that has been cut apart and resewn into a tube. You must first determine the size of the square you will need. To make approximately 400 inches of 2- or 2¼-inch-wide double-fold binding, enough to bind most bed quilts, start with a 30-inch square. If you don't have enough fabric for one large square, use several smaller squares. To estimate the number of inches of binding a particular square will produce, use this formula:

Multiply the length of one side by the length of another

side. Divide the result by the width of binding you want.

Using a 30-inch square and 2¼-inch binding as an example: 30 × 30 = 900; 900 ÷ 2¼ = 400 inches of binding.

Seven Steps to Continuous-Cut Binding

1. Once you have determined the size you need, measure and cut a square of fabric.

2. Fold the square in half diagonally and press lightly. Cut the square into two triangles, cutting on the fold line.

3. Place the two triangles, right sides together, as shown in **Diagram 29.** Sew the pieces together, taking a ¼-inch seam. Open out the two pieces and press the seam open. The resulting piece should look like the one shown in **Diagram 30.**

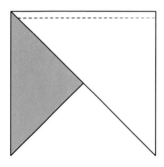

Diagram 29: Place the triangles right sides together as shown and stitch.

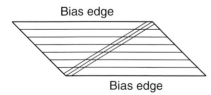

Diagram 30: Open out the two pieces and press the seam open. On the wrong side, mark cutting lines parallel to the bias edges.

4. Referring to **Diagram 30,** mark cutting lines on the wrong

side of the fabric in the desired binding width. Mark parallel to the bias edges.

5. Fold the fabric right sides together, bringing the two non-bias edges together and offsetting them by one strip width, as shown in **Diagram 31.** Pin the edges together, creating a tube, and sew, taking a ¼-inch seam. Press the seam open.

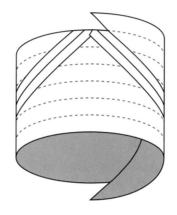

Diagram 31: Bring the nonbias edges together, offsetting them by one strip width. Sew the edges together to create a tube.

6. Cut on the marked lines, as shown in **Diagram 32,** turning the tube as you cut one long bias strip.

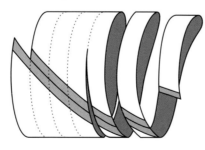

Diagram 32: Turning the tube as you go, cut along the marked lines to make one long bias strip.

7. To make double-fold binding, fold the long strip in half lengthwise, wrong sides together, and press.

Straight-Grain Binding

Straight-grain binding is easier to prepare than bias binding. Simply cut strips on the crosswise grain of the fabric and sew them together end to end with diagonal seams to get the required length. Although it isn't as flexible as bias binding, it is fine for straight-edge quilts.

Simple Straight-Grain Binding Method

1. Refer to the project instructions for the amount of binding the quilt requires. Estimate and cut the needed number of strips. When possible, cut the straight strips across the width of the fabric rather than along the length so they are slightly stretchy and easier to use.

2. Join the strips, as shown in **Diagram 33.** Place them right sides together, with each strip set in ¼ inch from the end of the other strip. Sew a diagonal seam. Trim the excess, leaving a ¼-inch seam. Continue adding strips until you have the length needed. For double-fold binding, fold and press the long strip in half lengthwise, with wrong sides together.

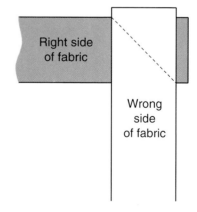

Diagram 33: Place the strips right sides together, positioning each strip ¼ inch in from the end of the other strip. Join with a diagonal seam.

Preparing a Quilt for Binding

Wait to trim excess batting and backing until after the binding is stitched to the top of the quilt. If the edges of the quilt are uneven after quilting, use a ruler and pencil to mark a placement line for the binding, as close as possible to the raw edges of the quilt top. This will give you a guideline against which you can align the raw edge of the binding strip. For best results, use a ruled square to mark the placement lines at the corners.

If you have a walking or even feed foot for your sewing machine, use it in place of the regular presser foot when sewing on the binding. If you do not have a walking foot, thread baste around the quilt along the edges to hold the layers firmly together during binding and to avoid puckers.

Attaching the Binding

1. Once you have made your binding strips (using either the continuous-cut bias or straight-grain strip method), you must prepare them so they can be attached to the quilt. If you are using double-fold binding, fold the long strip in half lengthwise, wrong sides together, and press. If you are using single-fold binding, you must fold over ¼ inch along one long side of the strip and press.

2. Begin attaching the binding in the middle of a side, not in a corner. Place the binding strip right sides together with the quilt top, with the raw edges of the binding strip even with the raw edge of the quilt top (or the drawn placement line).

3. Fold over the beginning raw edge of the binding approx-

imately 1 inch, as shown in **Diagram 34.** Securing the stitches with a backstitch, begin sewing ½ inch from the fold. Sew the binding to the quilt, stitching through all layers, ¼ inch from the raw edge of the binding.

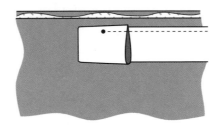

Diagram 34: Fold the raw edge back about 1 inch, and begin stitching ½ inch from the fold. Backstitch to anchor the stitching.

4. When you are approaching a corner, stop stitching exactly ¼ inch away from the raw edge of the corner. Backstitch and remove the quilt from the sewing machine, clipping threads.

5. Fold the binding up and away from the corner, as shown in **Diagram 35A,** forming a 45 degree angle fold.

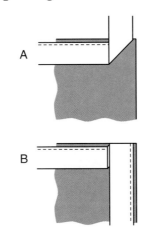

Diagram 35: Stop stitching ¼ inch from the corner and fold the binding up at a 45 degree angle (A). Fold the binding strip back down, align the raw edges with the side of the quilt top, and stitch the binding in place (B).

6. Fold the binding strip back down and align the raw edges with the adjacent side of the corner, as shown in **Diagram 35B.**

7. Begin stitching the next side at the top raw edge of the quilt, as shown in **Diagram 35B.** The fold created in the fabric is essential; it provides the fullness necessary to fit around the corners as you fold the binding to the back side of the quilt. Miter all four corners in this manner.

8. As you approach the point where you began, cross the folded-back beginning section with the ending section. Sew across the fold, as shown in **Diagram 36;** allow the end section to extend approximately ½ inch beyond the binding.

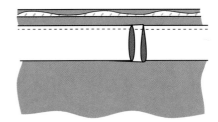

Diagram 36: Cross the beginning section with the ending section, overlapping them about ½ inch.

9. Trim away the excess batting and backing, using scissors or a rotary cutter and a ruler. Before you trim the whole quilt, fold over a small section and turn the binding to the back of the quilt to determine the right amount of excess to trim. The binding will look best and wear longer if it is filled rather than hollow.

10. Turn the binding to the back of the quilt and blindstitch the folded edge in place, covering the machine stitches with the folded edge. Finish the miters at the corners by folding in the adjacent sides on the back of the quilt and placing several stitches in the miter, as shown in **Diagram 37.** Add several stitches to the miters on the front in the same manner.

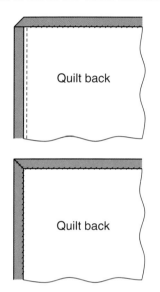

Diagram 37: Blindstitch the binding in place on the quilt back. Fold in the adjacent corner and stitch along the miter.

If you plan to add a hanging sleeve, follow the directions below to make and attach the sleeve before turning and finishing the binding.

Adding a Hanging Sleeve

If you plan to display your quilt, at home or at a quilt show, you will certainly need to add a hanging sleeve to the back.

The best way to prepare any of the wallhangings in this book for display is to add a hanging sleeve when you are binding the quilt. A rod or dowel can be inserted in the sleeve and supported by nails or hooks on the wall. Many quilters put hanging sleeves on bed quilts as well so that their work can be exhibited at quilt shows. Use the following procedure to add a 4-inch-wide hanging sleeve, which can accommodate a 24-inch-diameter dowel or pole.

1. Cut a strip of muslin or other fabric that is 8½ inches wide and 1 inch shorter than the width of the finished quilt.

2. Machine hem the short ends. To hem, turn under ½ inch on each end of the strip and press. Turn under another ½ inch and stitch next to the pressed fold.

3. Fold and press the strip in half lengthwise, wrong sides together, aligning the two long raw edges.

4. Position the raw edges of the sleeve to align with the top raw edges on the back of the quilt, centering the sleeve on the quilt. The binding should already be sewn on the front, but not turned to the back of the quilt. Pin the sleeve in place.

5. Machine stitch the sleeve to the back of the quilt, stitching from the front by sewing on top of the stitches that hold the binding to the quilt.

6. Turn the binding to the back of the quilt and hand stitch it in place so that the binding covers the raw edge of the sleeve, as shown in **Diagram 38.** When turning the binding on the edge that has the sleeve, you may need to trim away more batting and backing in order to turn the binding easily.

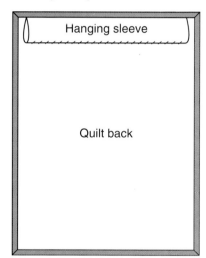

Diagram 38: Stitch the raw edge of the sleeve to the top of the quilt. Bring the binding to the back of the quilt and hand stitch it in place, covering the top raw edge of the sleeve. Then, hand stitch the bottom edge of the sleeve to the quilt back.

7. Hand stitch the bottom loose edge of the sleeve in place, being careful not to sew through to the front of the quilt.

Directory of Quilt Shows

Because the dates and locations for many quilt shows change from year to year, and because there are new shows being added to the calendar all the time, it is impossible to provide a complete and current listing. The shows listed here are national in scope and therefore generally have fixed locations and dates. Write to the addresses provided for exact dates and complete information.

American Quilter's Society National Quilt Show and Contest

Paducah, Kentucky
Date: Generally in late April
Mailing address:
American Quilter's Society
P.O. Box 3290
Paducah, KY 42002-3290

The Great American Quilt Festival

New York City
Date: Generally in early May
Mailing address:
Museum of American Folk Art
Quilt Connection
61 West 62nd Street
New York, NY 10023

International Quilt Festival

Houston, Texas
Date: Generally the last week in October
Mailing address:
International Quilt Festival
14520 Memorial Drive #54
Houston, TX 77079

Mid-Atlantic Quilt Festival

Williamsburg, Virginia
Date: Generally the last week in February
Mailing address:
Mid-Atlantic Quilt Festival
c/o David M. & Peter J. Mancuso, Inc.
P.O. Box 667
New Hope, PA 18938

National Quilting Association

The location and date change each year for the NQA show, though it is always held during the summer.
Mailing address:
National Quilting Association
P.O. Box 393
Ellicott City, MD 21041-0393

Pacific International Quilt Festival

San Francisco, California
Date: Generally the second week in October
Mailing address:
P.I.Q.F.
c/o David M. & Peter J. Mancuso, Inc.
P.O. Box 667
New Hope, PA 18938

Quilters' Heritage Celebration

Lancaster, Pennsylvania
Date: Generally the first week in April
Mailing address:
Quilters' Heritage Celebration
P.O. Box 503
Carlinville, IL 62626

Silver Dollar City's National Quilt Festival

Branson, Missouri
Date: Generally late August or early September
Mailing address:
Special Events Department
Silver Dollar City, Inc.
West Highway 76
Branson, MO 65616

Your Quilt Could Be Published!

Imagine your quilt in a future volume of *America's Best Quilting Projects!* All you have to do is send us a photograph of your project. If the Rodale Press editors choose your project for inclusion in a future volume, you will be paid for the use of your quilt and get a copy of the book free!

Send slides or photos of as many quilts or quilting projects as you like. We're interested in original designs, based on a traditional style. We're also interested in classic quilt designs with interesting color combinations or some sort of special, unique touch. Projects can include bed quilts, wallhangings, and smaller quilted projects such as home accessories and gift items.

Tell us a little about your project (or projects): What inspired it? What techniques did you use? Did you make it for someone special? Has it appeared in any shows or won any awards?

So show us what you've done! Send a slide or photo that clearly shows your project to:

Jane Townswick
Rodale Press, Inc.
33 East Minor Street
Emmaus, PA 18098-0099

Whether we choose your project or not, all slides and photos will be returned to you.